DEPLOY
THAT FABRIC

23 Sewing Projects Use Military Uniforms in Everyday Life

Jen Eskridge

stash BOOKS®

an imprint of C&T Publishing

Text copyright © 2011 by Jen Eskridge

Photography and Artwork copyright © 2011 by C&T Publishing, Inc.

Publisher: Amy Marson

Creative Director: Gailen Runge

Acquisitions Editor: Susanne Woods

Editor: Lynn Koolish

Technical Editors: Ellen Pahl, Sandy Peterson, and Gailen Runge

Cover/Book Designer: Kristy Zacharias

Page Layout Artist: April Mostek

Production Coordinator: Jessica Jenkins

Production Editor: Alice Mace Nakanishi

Illustrator: Aliza Shalit

Photography by Christina Carty-Francis and Diane Pedersen of C&T Publishing, Inc., unless otherwise noted

Published by Stash Books, an imprint of C&T Publishing, Inc., P.O. Box 1456, Lafayette, CA 94549

Library of Congress Cataloging-in-Publication Data

Eskridge, Jen (Jennifer Reanna)

Deploy That Fabric : 23 Sewing Projects Use Military Uniforms in Everyday Life / Jen Eskridge.

   pages cm

ISBN 978-1-60705-244-9 (soft cover)

1. Clothing and dress--Remaking. 2. Military uniforms. I. Title.

TT550.E85 2011

646'.3--dc22

2010048433

Printed in China

10 9 8 7 6 5 4 3 2 1

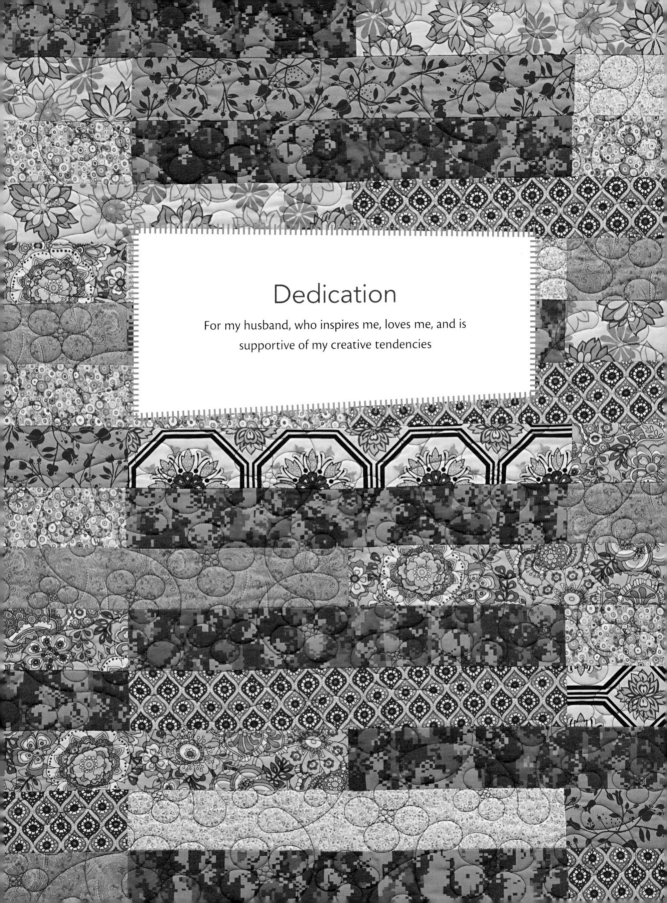

Dedication

For my husband, who inspires me, loves me, and is
supportive of my creative tendencies

Acknowledgments

Thank you to our military service members—the men and women who defend our freedoms and protect our way of life.

This book evolved from a simple idea into a complete book. None of it would have been possible without the pattern testers—Karen Morello, Becky Morello, Colleen Eskridge, Leigh Roper, Dawn Owens, Debbie Fick, Annette Miller, Nicole Gustafson, Kathy Schwabeland, and Joann Farely. Thank you so much for your support and ideas.

Thank you also to the companies that generously donated fabric and supplies for the projects in this book: FreeSpirit Fabrics, Michael Miller Fabrics, Blank Quilting, Art Gallery Fabrics, Superior Threads, and C&T Publishing.

Note

This book is not endorsed by any branch or member of the U.S. military.

CONTENTS

8   INTRODUCTION

9   USING UNIFORMS
     • *Deconstructing a Uniform into Flat Pieces* • *Uniform Weights* • *Washing and Pressing* • *Patches and Embellishments* • *Choosing Matching Fabrics* • *Cutting* • *Equivalent Yardages*

PROJECTS

15   PURSES AND TOTES

16   Hipster Purse

20   Grocery Tote

23   Coin Purse

25   Makeup Bag

28   Grommet Purse

34   Half-Moon Purse

39   Reversible Tote

44   Circle Purse

51   Military Monster Tote

57   HOME FOR THE HOLIDAYS

58   Placemats

60   Stocking

64   Tree Skirt

68   Table Runner

71   QUILTS AND BABY ITEMS

72   Stroller Blanket

75   Changing Pad

78   Triangle Jubilee

83   Sensational Strips

86   ACCESSORIES

87   Note Cards

89   Drink Coasters

92   Business Card Holder

94   Checkbook Cover

97   Passport Cover

99   Accent Pillow

102   SEWING AND QUILTING TECHNIQUES

102   Grainlines

102   Edge Stitching

103   Quilted Handles

104   Bag-Shaping Darts

105   Hard-Bottom Bag Insert

106   Welt Pocket

109   Zipper Pocket

111   Center-Applied Zipper

113   Center-Applied Zipper with Lining

116   Quilt Finishing
      Layering · Basting · Quilting · Binding · Labels

120   TEMPLATE PATTERNS

127   ABOUT THE AUTHOR

INTRODUCTION

The main purpose of this book is to honor the service members who are fighting for our freedoms, both at home and abroad. Of course, an added bonus is that by using the tips, tricks, and projects in this book, you can also recycle military uniforms after they are no longer needed for service.

Although I wholly advocate recycling used, stained, ripped, or decommissioned uniforms, it is very important to ask your service member first before you sneak garments out of the back of the closet.

Deploy That Fabric is organized in three sections.

The first section describes tips and techniques for deconstructing and repurposing a uniform.

The next section is a collection of projects made using the military uniform paired with bright, colorful fabrics. Projects range from accessories and home décor to holiday and baby items. The projects require varying degrees of sewing skill; the level is indicated at the beginning of the project. Skill levels, which range from novice to skilled to experienced, are defined as follows:

- ★ **Novice:** Beginner

- ★★ **Skilled:** Confident beginner

- ★★★ **Experienced:** Intermediate sewer with considerable experience

The final section contains sewing and quilting techniques. This section explains the techniques you will need to make the projects in this book, as well as for other sewing projects you undertake.

If you are apprehensive about cutting into your service member's uniform, consider purchasing a uniform from a thrift store. It may be easier to start a project if you aren't emotionally attached to the fabric. What's important is that you are making the project for someone you care about. Also, keep in mind that the uniform you are using is no longer needed, so anything you make will breathe new life into it. Go forth and create with confidence. You can do it!

USING UNIFORMS

Deconstructing a Uniform into Flat Pieces

The most important element in preparing your uniform for repurposing is to create flat pieces that will be easy to work with. Clothing often has shape-fitting darts or curved seams to control the fit of the garment, and a uniform is no different. Cut around these curves or rip out the stitching line to create flat, usable pieces. The shapes that you end up with may be very odd, but that's okay.

Note ★ *At the time of this writing, military uniforms are as described. By the time the book is released and future copies are read, some variations may have been introduced to the ever-changing military uniform.* ★

Uniforms have many stitching lines, seams, and reinforced areas that you can use to your advantage. For example, there is no reason to unstitch or rip out the traditional reinforced welt seams found on most uniforms, as these seams provide a distinct pieced look to the overall fabric. When a pattern calls for a piece of fabric larger than what is available from the original breakdown, you can join smaller pieces. Sewing two uniform pieces together and then edge-stitching (page 102) the seam with coordinating thread can easily help you achieve a look similar to the original uniform seams.

Here are some helpful hints when working with uniforms.

○ Use your seam ripper carefully. Uniforms are sewn and fortified for durable wear in the field, which means it will take some muscle power to rip out stitches, particularly tack stitches around the sleeve and front closure areas.

○ Cut to the right and left of any major seamlines, rather than ripping them with a seam ripper.

○ Collars, cuffs, and waistbands do not provide enough usable material, so don't bother with these parts.

○ Be sure to save zippers, buttons, nametapes, and so on.

○ Always remove reinforcing layers. Doing so will reduce bulk and make the fabric easier to sew. Reinforced areas are generally at the knees, elbows, and buttocks.

○ If you don't plan to use pockets as functioning pockets, consider sewing them closed and removing the fabric from behind the pocket area.

○ If you need a small extra piece of fabric, the pants pockets at the waist are often lined with uniform fabric. Simply cut these pieces away from the pants and press them open and flat.

○ When working with scraps, you may find that the perfect-sized scrap actually spans a curved uniform seam. You can still use this piece by folding a triangular shape of fabric, or dart, into the fabric behind the curved seam. Sew over the existing seam to hold the dart in place. This will make your piece usable and flat.

DECONSTRUCTING A UNIFORM

1. Cut along shirt side seams.
2. Cut off sleeves.
3. Cut sleeves open.
4. Cut off shirt collar.
5. Cut off shirt placket.
6. Cut off shirt cuffs.
7. Cut along pant side seams.
8. Cut along pant inseams.
9. Cut off pant waistband.
10. Cut off pant hem.
11. Remove and save any zippers.

USING UNIFORMS

Uniform Weights

Military uniforms are made from a variety of weights of fabric. The lighter-weight fabrics have a softer drape and are easier to sew.

As with all sewing, select the appropriate needle size for the weight of the fabric. For lightweight uniforms and quilting or home décor fabric, use a size 14 needle. For heavier-weight uniforms and denim fabric, use a size 16 needle.

When sewing uniform fabric, be advised that not only will you be sewing a heavier-weight fabric, but you will also be layering it to create seams. This may cause even the strongest needle to break. Your sewing machine may not want to push through the stiff layers. Be patient, take your time, and use the flywheel to turn the needle by hand if your sewing machine is giving you trouble.

Washing and Pressing

Prewash uniforms to remove starch or any other fabric coatings or sizing. Iron out the wrinkles using a hot iron with steam.

Used uniforms will have been washed and dried many times, so you can be confident that there will be no shrinkage.

Uniforms can withstand ironing on the highest heat for all projects. When working on projects, keep in mind the ironing requirements of the other fabrics. All the projects in this book are made with 100% cotton that can be ironed with a hot iron and steam.

The purses and bags are best spot cleaned only. All other projects can be machine washed and dried.

Patches and Embellishments

Some of the most favored embellishments for your repurposed designs are the service member's actual patches from the original uniform. Use a seam ripper to remove these patches. Reapply them to your project in a location that is pleasing to you.

Buttons are another fun embellishment. With some projects, you can use the original uniform buttons intact in the design. In other cases, you may choose to remove the buttons and reapply them where they work best in your design.

I do not advocate using rank on repurposed projects unless you either use all the ranks the service member earned during his or her career or use the retirement or final rank earned. For the most part, these projects are for the service member's support network—that is, individuals who are not necessarily military personnel. However, I do enjoy the idea of sewing general's insignia on baby items, since we know it's the baby who runs the house. Remember, this is your project, and

you are the one who will carry it or gift it. The embellishment details are completely up to you.

To further personalize your project, consider adding nonmilitary patches to the design. Another idea is to sew hook-and-loop tape to existing patches and add them to hook-and-loop tape areas on the original uniform. Vintage brooches are a nonmilitary embellishment that can add shiny, high-contrast bling to any uniform project.

Nametapes are a critical part of the military uniform. Many people recycling uniforms choose to use the name either in place on the uniform or as it would traditionally look on the uniform. You may also consider wild, punchy nametapes to match your personality. When sewing your project, plan to add the nametape during the sewing process, rather than at the very end.

  TIP   Though every military installation has its embroidery shop, you might consider having a nametape custom made at a local nonmilitary embroidery shop. Embroidery shops have many more color options and can vary the nametape length to accommodate much longer words or phrases. They can also provide, in many cases, different fonts.

Choosing Matching Fabrics

What matches a uniform? Everything. Treat the uniform as a neutral color. From there, decide which colors you want to use for a particular project. Choose bright, bold fabrics to contrast with the subdued uniform colors. Or choose a specific line of fabrics at your quilt shop or fabric store, because you know these fabrics are already going to match and complement one another.

Now that you know that almost any fabric can go with a uniform, the key to success is to treat the uniform as a "light" or a "dark." All colors and fabrics have values—light, medium, and dark. These values are always relative. This color value assignment is most critical in quilting projects, though high contrast in all projects is what makes them unique and fun.

Although pairing uniform fabric with fabric of a similar weight is ideal, doing so is not always possible. In many projects in this book, matching the weight of the uniform isn't critical. If you feel that you need to match the weight of the uniform fabric, fuse medium-weight fusible interfacing, such as Shape-Flex (by C&T Publishing), to the back of the lighter-weight cotton. This should give the fabric the same weight as the uniform.

TIP Recycled uniform fabric has been washed and dried many times, so it isn't going to shrink, and the colors won't run. The same can't be said for all your purchased fabric. Therefore, it's important to prewash all coordinating cotton print or military yardage to prevent any uneven shrinking of a project should you need to wash it later on.

Cutting

When planning the cutting for the flat pieces of uniform fabric, make sure you don't have a heavy welt seam in any of the seam allowances. As much as possible, plan to have uniform welt seams perpendicular to any project seams.

If you use a rotary cutter, be aware that the uniform pieces will dull the blade quicker than commercial cottons. It may also be difficult to cut through heavy welt seams, pockets, and other thick areas.

TIP If you've never used a rotary cutter before, ask about techniques at your local fabric or quilt shop, refer to a book for beginning quilters, or look online for basic how-to information.

Freezer-paper templates are a good option for cutting large or unusual shapes. Draw or copy the template patterns onto the paper side of the freezer paper, cut out the templates, and iron the templates (shiny side down) to the appropriate fabrics.

After the paper is in place, use a rotary cutter or sharp fabric scissors to cut out along the edge of the freezer paper. You can reuse the freezer-paper templates up to seven times.

No matter which method of cutting you choose, you will still need to plan where the unique uniform elements, such as pockets and nametapes, will fall. Sometimes the elements will be centered and perfect; other times, they will be more "creatively" placed.

Equivalent Yardages

The yardages provided in the projects are ballpark estimates of how much usable fabric is in a uniform (based on standard 42"-wide fabric).

✪ Most shirts provide about ⅔ yard, though the bulky pocket area may not always be usable.

✪ Most pants provide about 1 yard of flat fabric.

PURSES
* AND *
TOTES

HIPSTER PURSE

SKILLED

Just the right size and quick to sew.

Finished size: 7˝ wide × 10˝ high × 1˝ deep | **Needle:** Size 14

Materials and Supplies

1 pair of military uniform pants (or scraps) or ¼ yard military-style fabric

¼ yard cotton print fabric

½ yard 20″-wide Shape-Flex fusible interfacing

1½ yards 1¼″-wide webbing or thick twill tape for strap*

Magnetic clasp**

Craft knife (for magnet clasp installation)

Uniform button (*optional*)

Since this bag is designed to be worn across the body, you may need to shorten or lengthen the strap depending on the fit. A Quilted Handle (page 103) may be substituted for the twill tape if desired; if so, you'll need an extra ¼ yard of fabric or scraps to total ¼ yard.

**Look for these in the notions section of your favorite fabric store, where other purse hardware and accessories are located.*

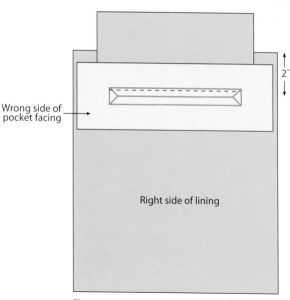

Sewing and Quilting TECHNIQUES

Welt Pocket (page 106)

Quilted Handles (*optional, page 103*)

Cutting

UNIFORM FABRIC

- Cut 2 rectangles 8″ × 11″ for purse.

COTTON PRINT FABRIC

- Cut 2 rectangles 8″ × 11″ for lining.
- Cut 1 rectangle 4½″ × 5″ for pocket flap.
- Cut 1 rectangle 6″ × 10″ for pocket lining.
- Cut 1 rectangle 2″ × 6″ for pocket facing.

FUSIBLE INTERFACING

- Cut 2 rectangles 8″ × 11″.
- Cut 1 rectangle 2″ × 6″ for pocket facing.

Construction

Seam allowances are ½″, unless otherwise noted.

Exterior and Lining Pieces

1. Apply a Welt Pocket (page 106) to one of the uniform fabric rectangles. The pocket should be 2″ below the top 8″-wide edge. (Figure 1)

2″

Wrong side of pocket facing

Right side of lining

Figure 1

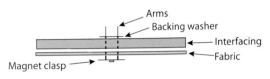

Figure 2

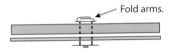

Figure 3

Figure 4

2. Fuse the interfacing to the wrong side of the lining rectangles, following the manufacturer's directions.

Magnetic Clasp

1. With a water-soluble pen, mark the clasp placement so it is centered 1½″ down from the top lining edge.

2. Use a craft knife to make 2 small slits (through the lining and interfacing) the width of the magnet clasp "arms" on each side of the marked location.

3. Place the arms of the male magnet clasp through the slits from the right side of the lining piece. Put the washer over the arms from the interfacing side, sandwiching the interfacing and lining between the metal pieces. (Figure 2)

4. Using pliers, fold each arm of the clasp down around the washer. Make the arms as flat as possible. (Figure 3)

5. Repeat Steps 1–4 with the female side of the magnet clasp on the opposite side of the lining.

Finishing

1. If you plan to add nametapes, patches, or embellishments to the bag exterior, now is the time.

2. Place the uniform rectangles right sides together, matching raw edges. Sew around the right, left, and bottom sides with a ½″ seam allowance.

3. Repeat Step 2 with the lining. (Figure 4)

Note: If you've opted to make a Quilted Handle (page 103), make it now.

HIPSTER PURSE

4. Position the handle ends right sides together on the bag exterior so they are centered over the side seam. Align the raw edges and baste in place ¼" from the edge. (Figure 5)

5. Fold the top edges of the lining and the exterior ½" toward the wrong side of the bag. Press.

6. Turn the lining wrong side out. Turn the bag exterior right side out. Place the lining into the exterior with wrong sides together. Align the top edges and match the side seams. Pin the bag and lining together.

7. Edge-stitch (page 102) around the top to secure the exterior to the lining. Make sure the handle is up and out of the way. (Figure 6)

8. Center a decorative button on the pocket flap (*optional*).

TIP Consider adding ribbon to the handle, as described in the Military Monster Tote project (page 56).

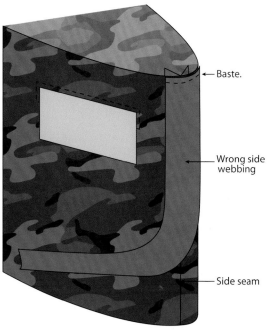

Baste.

Wrong side webbing

Side seam

Figure 5

Figure 6

GROCERY TOTE

NOVICE

The perfect size for the market,
doctor's office, or craft night.

Finished size: 9˝ wide × 11½˝ high × 6˝ deep | **Needle:** Size 14

Materials and Supplies

Military uniform scraps* or ¼ yard military-style fabric

1⅛ yards cotton print fabric

1 yard 22"-wide fast2fuse interfacing (by C&T Publishing)

1 yard 1"-wide grosgrain ribbon

⅔ yard ½"-wide grosgrain ribbon

1" × 28" piece of dense batting for quilted handles

6" × 9" piece of matboard or cardboard

1½"-diameter decorative brooch (optional)

*You can piece scraps to make 2 rectangles at least 6½" × 14½".

Sewing and Quilting TECHNIQUES

Quilted Handles (page 103)

Bag-Shaping Darts (page 104)

Hard-Bottom Bag Insert (page 105)

Cutting

UNIFORM FABRIC

- Cut 2 rectangles 6½" × 14½" for bottom exterior.

COTTON PRINT FABRIC

- Cut 2 rectangles 9½" × 14½" for upper exterior.
- Cut 2 rectangles 14½" × 15½" for lining.
- Cut 2 strips 3" × 14" for handles.*
- Cut 2 rectangles 6½" × 9½" for bag insert.

FAST2FUSE INTERFACING

- Cut 2 rectangles 15½" × 14½".

BATTING

- Cut 2 strips 1" × 14" for handles.*

*You can cut these 28" long if you want handles that will go over your shoulder. Cut the batting strips to the same length.

Construction

Seam allowances are ½", unless otherwise noted.

Exterior and Lining

1. Place the uniform rectangles, right sides together, on the cotton print rectangles for the upper exterior. Sew along the 14½" side using a ¼" seam allowance. Press the seam allowances toward the cotton print. (Figure 1)

2. Place the 1"-wide ribbon over the seam on the bag exterior pieces from Step 1. Edge-stitch (page 102) the ribbon to the bag and trim the ribbon to match the bag width.

Figure 1

Figure 2

3. Fuse the fast2fuse interfacing to the wrong side of the bag exterior pieces, following the manufacturer's directions.

4. Place the bag exteriors right sides together, lining up the ribbon detail and seams. Sew around the right, bottom, and left sides of the bag.

5. Place the lining pieces right sides together. Sew around the sides and bottom. Leave a 5″ gap in the stitching along the bottom so you can turn the bag right side out when the construction is finished. (Figure 2)

Finishing

1. Make the Bag-Shaping Darts (page 104) on the lining and bag exterior. Make the dart 3″ from the triangle tip. (Figure 3)

2. Make the 14″-long Quilted Handles (page 103).

3. Align the raw edges of the handles with the raw edge of the bag exterior, 2″ from the side seamlines. Machine baste a scant ¼″ from the top edge of the bag. Cut the ½″ ribbon into 2 pieces each 12″ long. Baste one end of each ribbon in the center along the top of the bag exterior. (Figure 4)

4. Turn the bag exterior inside out and the bag lining right side out. Place the lining into the exterior with right sides together. Pin the 2 pieces together along the top edge, matching seam allowances on the sides. Sew around the top edge.

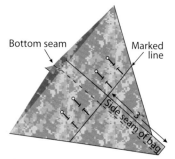

Figure 3

5. Turn the bag right side out through the opening in the lining. Press the top seam.

6. Pin around the top to hold the interfacing in place; edge-stitch around the top.

7. Press the entire bag.

8. Sew the opening in the bag lining by hand or machine.

Figure 4

9. Make a Hard-Bottom Bag Insert (page 105).

10. Pin a brooch to the bag, if desired, centering it on the ribbon in the front.

COIN PURSE

Sewing and Quilting
TECHNIQUES

Center-Applied Zipper with Lining
(page 113)

Ease into sewing and zippers
with this small coin purse project.
It's quick to finish and enjoy.

Finished size: 4″ × 3½″ | **Needle:** Size 14

★
★

SKILLED

Materials and Supplies

Military uniform scraps or 1 fat eighth military-style fabric	7″ plastic nonseparating zipper
1 fat eighth cotton print fabric or assorted fabric scraps	½ yard ⅜″-wide satin or grosgrain ribbon

Figure 1   Make 4.

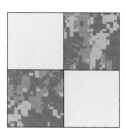

Make 2.

Figure 2

Cutting

RIBBON

❂ Cut 3 pieces 5″ long.

UNIFORM FABRIC

❂ Cut 4 squares 2½″ × 2½″.

COTTON PRINT FABRIC

❂ Cut 4 squares 2½″ × 2½″ for exterior.

❂ Cut 2 squares 4½″ × 4½″ for lining.

Construction

Seam allowances are ¼″, unless otherwise noted.

1. Place the uniform squares and cotton print squares right sides together; sew. Press the seam allowances toward the cotton print. Make 4 pairs. (Figure 1)

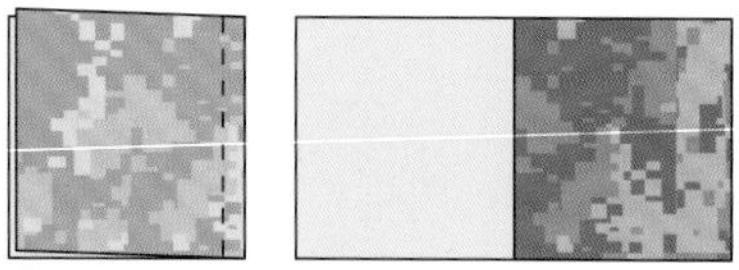

2. Make a checkerboard Four-Patch by sewing together 2 pairs of squares, matching the center seam. Press the seam allowances to one side. (Don't worry if the seamlines don't match perfectly; they will be covered by the ribbon.) (Figure 2)

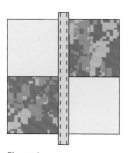

Figure 3

3. Place a piece of ribbon over the center seamline of each Four-Patch and edge-stitch (page 102) in place to cover the seam. (Figure 3)

4. Fold the last length of ribbon in half. Baste the raw edges to the top left side of a Four-Patch, ¾″ from the top raw edge. (Figure 4)

5. Insert a Center-Applied Zipper with Lining (page 113) using a ½″ seam allowance. Note that the zipper ends will need to be tacked closed, because the zipper is longer than the purse's top edge.

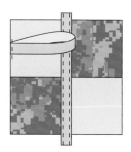

Figure 4

6. Turn the bag right side out and push the corners into place with a blunt object. Sew the opening in the lining closed.

COIN PURSE

MAKEUP BAG

Functional, fast, and fun.

Finished size: 7½″ wide x 6″ high x 3″ deep | **Needle:** Size 14

★
★★
SKILLED

Materials and Supplies

Assorted military uniform scraps or 1 fat eighth military-style fabric

1 fat quarter cotton print fabric or assorted fabric scraps

9" plastic nonseparating zipper

Turning tool, such as Dritz Loop Turner or Fasturn

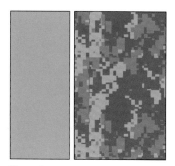

Figure 1

Cutting

UNIFORM FABRIC

- ✪ Cut 2 rectangles 5½" × 8½" for exterior.

COTTON PRINT FABRIC

- ✪ Cut 2 rectangles 3½" × 8½" for exterior.
- ✪ Cut 2 squares 8½" × 8½" for lining.
- ✪ Cut 1 rectangle 2" × 8" for handle.

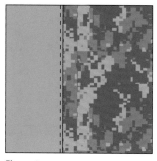

Figure 2

Construction

Seam allowances are ¼", unless otherwise noted.

1. Place the 3½" × 8½" cotton pieces on the 5½" × 8½" uniform pieces with right sides together. Sew along the 8½" sides. Press the seam allowances toward the cotton print. (Figure 1)

2. Edge-stitch (page 102) along the seamline on the cotton print side. (Figure 2)

MAKEUP BAG

3. Fold the 2″ × 8″ rectangle in half lengthwise with right sides together. Sew along the length to form a tube for the handle.

4. Use a turning tool to turn the tube right side out. Press with the seam allowance centered on the back of the tube. (Figure 3)

Figure 3

5. Fold the tube in half and position it ¾″ from the top on the left side of the exterior, aligning the raw edges. Baste in place. (Figure 4)

6. Insert a Center-Applied Zipper with Lining (page 113) using a ½″ seam allowance. The zipper pull should be next to the side with the handle.

7. Make Bag-Shaping Darts (page 104) on the lower edges of the lining and exterior pieces 1½″ from the corner.

8. Turn the bag right side out. Push the corners into place with a blunt object. Sew the opening in the lining closed.

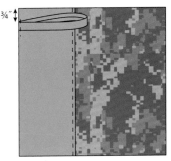

¾″

Figure 4

Sewing and Quilting
TECHNIQUES

Center-Applied Zipper with Lining (page 113)

Bag-Shaping Darts (page 104)

GROMMET PURSE

★ ★

SKILLED

Jazz up a uniform with high-contrast ribbon and fabric on this impressively stylish, deceptively easy-to-sew purse.

Finished size: 11½″ wide × 10″ high × 4″ deep | **Needle:** Size 14

Materials and Supplies

1 military uniform shirt or ¾ yard military-style fabric

1⅛ yards cotton print fabric for lining, handles, and purse sides

1 yard 20″-wide Shape-Flex fusible interfacing

4 grommets 1″ in diameter

Grommet-setting tools (*if needed*)

7″ plastic nonseparating zipper

1½ yards 1″-wide grosgrain ribbon

Cutting

Template patterns are on pages 124–126. For the bag pattern, see Making the Template (at right).

UNIFORM FABRIC

- ✿ Cut 1 using bag template.
- ✿ Cut 2 using side panel template.
- ✿ Cut 2 using pocket template.

LINING FABRIC

- ✿ Cut 1 using bag template.
- ✿ Cut 2 using side panel template.
- ✿ Cut 2 using pocket template.
- ✿ Cut 1 piece 10″ × 40″ and 1 piece 10″ × 14″ for handle.
- ✿ Cut 1 piece 2″ × 10″ for zipper facing.
- ✿ Cut 1 piece 8″ × 10″ for zipper pocket lining.

INTERFACING

- ✿ Cut 1 using bag template.
- ✿ Cut 2 using side panel template.

Sewing and Quilting
TECHNIQUES
Zipper Pocket (page 109)

Making the Template

To make a freezer-paper template for the bag, cut a piece of freezer paper 26″ long and fold it in half across the width. From the fold, draw 3 sides of a rectangle 7¾″ × 12½″, referring to the template diagram (below). Trace the partial pattern for the top of the bag (page 124) and place it along the 12½″ side of the drawn rectangle. Trace and then flip the pattern to complete the curved top edge. Cut out the 2 layers of the paper along the drawn lines. Open up and you'll have the complete bag template.

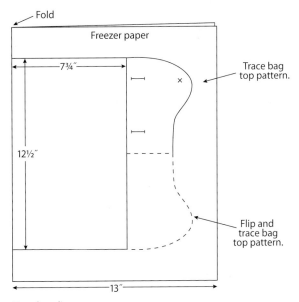

Template diagram

GROMMET PURSE

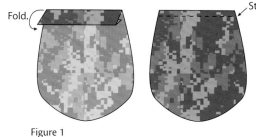

Fold.

Stitch.

Figure 1

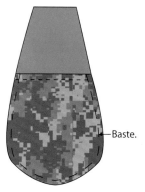

Baste.

Figure 2

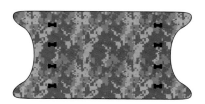

Figure 3

Construction

Seam allowances are ½", unless otherwise noted.

Lining

1. Iron the fusible interfacing to the wrong side of the bag lining and side panel lining, following the manufacturer's directions.

2. Insert a Zipper Pocket (page 109) into the lining where indicated on the pattern.

Side Pockets

1. Hem the side pocket pieces cut from military fabric by folding over the top edge ¼" twice. Sew across the top edge of each pocket piece. (Figure 1)

2. Place a hemmed pocket onto each side panel of contrasting fabric, matching the lower curved edges. Machine baste the layers together along the curved edge. (Figure 2)

3. Repeat Steps 1 and 2 for the pocket pieces cut from cotton print.

Assembling

Sort the bag pieces into exterior pieces and lining pieces. Each set should include 1 bag and 2 prepared side panels. Work with one set of pieces at a time, so your side panels do not become mixed up.

1. Make 1¼"-long buttonholes on the bag exterior at the marked locations. (Figure 3)

 TIP

 If your machine does not have an automatic buttonhole feature, make a very narrow, short zigzag stitch down the right and left sides of the marked location.

 At the top and bottom of the parallel zigzag lines, make a very wide zigzag tack stitch, giving the look of a traditional buttonhole. Carefully cut the buttonhole openings.

2. If you are adding any nametapes or additional patches to the bag, add them now, before you sew the side panels on the bag.

3. Fold the bag exterior in half and make a small crease to locate the center of the bottom. Place the bag exterior and the side panel right sides together with centers aligned. Pin together. (Figure 4)

4. Pin the bag and side panel together, easing the bag around the lower curved edge. Pin closely to eliminate puckers or folds when sewing. Sew the bag to the side panel so the side panel is facing up; begin and end your stitching at the dots, backstitching at both points. Repeat this step for the opposite side panel. Press the seam allowances toward the side panels. (Figure 5)

5. Cut notches around the curved seam to minimize bulk when the bag is turned right side out. Be careful not to cut into the stitching. (Figure 6)

6. Repeat Steps 3–5 to add the side panels to the lining.

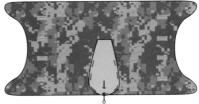

Pin at center.

Figure 4

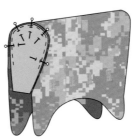

Figure 5

Figure 6

GROMMET PURSE

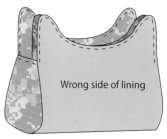

Wrong side of lining

Figure 7

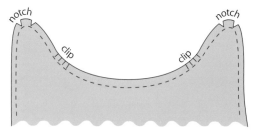

notch   notch

clip   clip

Figure 8

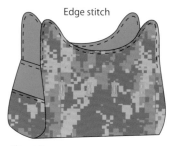

Edge stitch

Figure 9

Figure 10

7. Turn the bag exterior right side out. Turn the bag lining wrong side out.

8. Place the bag exterior into the bag lining. Pin the pieces together along the top edge. Match the curved shapes and the side panel seams.

9. Sew around the top edge, leaving a 4"–6" opening at the center back. Stop with the needle down and pivot the bag around the needle at the side panel seams. Backstitch at the starting and stopping points. (Figure 7)

10. Clip and notch around the curves along the top edge of the bag. (Figure 8)

11. Turn the bag right side out through the opening. Press the seam allowances of the opening to the wrong side by ½"; pin.

12. Edge-stitch (page 102) all around the top edge. (Figure 9)

Finishing

1. Carefully cut holes for the grommets. Attach the grommets, following the manufacturer's instructions. (Figure 10)

Figure 11

2. Sew the 2 handle pieces together along the short ends. Cut a 52"-long piece of fabric. Fold under an end by ½" and press. Fold the handle in half lengthwise, right sides together. Sew using a ¼" seam allowance down the entire length of the handle. (Figure 11)

3. Turn the handle right side out. Insert the handle through the grommet holes. (Figure 12)

4. Insert the raw edge of the handle into the folded end of the handle by about ½". Match the seam allowances and pin the 2 ends together. Stitch the handle ends together using a straight stitch; backstitch at the beginning and end. (Figure 13)

5. Weave the ribbon in and out through the buttonholes in the bag exterior. Tie the ribbon in a bow at the center front. Trim the ends to the desired length.

Figure 12

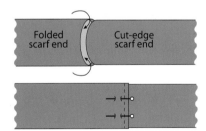

Folded scarf end   Cut-edge scarf end

Figure 13

HALF-MOON PURSE

★
★

SKILLED

Funky, fresh, and full of hip.

Finished size: 15½˝ wide × 6¼˝ high × 2˝ deep | **Needle:** Size 14

Sewing and Quilting
TECHNIQUES

Zipper Pocket (page 109)

Materials and Supplies

1 military uniform shirt or ½ yard military-style fabric

1 yard cotton print fabric for handle straps, lining, and purse bottom

½ yard medium-weight 20″-wide fusible interfacing

¾ yard 22″-wide fast2fuse interfacing (by C&T Publishing)

7″ plastic nonseparating zipper

⅞″ silver metal swivel hook*

⅞″ silver metal D-ring*

*Look for these in the notions section of your favorite fabric store, where other purse hardware and accessories are located.

Cutting

Template pattern is on page 123. For cutting with freezer-paper templates, see page 14.

UNIFORM FABRIC

○ Cut 2 using half-moon template.

COTTON PRINT FABRIC

○ Cut 2 using half-moon template.

○ Cut 2 strips 5″ × width of fabric; from 1 of the strips cut:

   1 strip 5″ × 12″ for shoulder strap

   1 strip 2″ × 10″ for zipper facing

   1 strip 2¼″ × 15″ for hardware strap

○ Cut 2 strips 2½″ × 26″ for purse bottom and lining.

○ Cut 1 piece 8″ × 10″ for zipper pocket lining.

FUSIBLE INTERFACING

○ Cut 1 strip 4½″ × 49½″ for handle interfacing.*

FAST2FUSE

○ Cut 2 using half-moon template.

○ Cut 1 strip 2½″ × 26″ for purse bottom.

*Cut the interfacing in sections and butt the ends together on the fabric when fusing.

Wrong side of handle fabric

Interfacing (fusible side down)

Figure 1

Figure 2

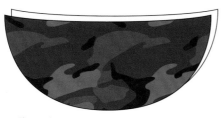

Fold

Figure 3

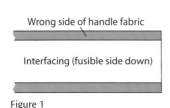

Figure 4

Construction

Seam allowances are ½", unless otherwise noted.

Handle

1. Place the 5" × 42" strip of cotton print and the 5" × 12" cotton print handle piece right sides together along the 5" edge. Sew using a ¼" seam allowance. Press. Trim this unit to 49½" long.

2. Place the fabric handle piece on the ironing board, wrong side up. Center the handle interfacing pieces (*fusible side down*) on the wrong side of the fabric and fuse the interfacing according to the manufacturer's directions. (Figure 1)

3. Press the remaining ¼" of fabric along the top and bottom of the interfacing toward the middle of the handle. (Figure 2)

4. Fold the entire handle piece in half lengthwise and press. Topstitch the right and left sides of the handle ¼" from the long edges. (Figure 3)

Interfacing

Note: If you want to add nametapes or patches to the uniform fabric, add them now, before adding the interfacing.

1. Center the half-moon uniform fabric pieces right side up on top of the half-moon pieces of fast2fuse interfacing. Fuse the fast2fuse to the wrong side of the uniform following the manufacturer's instructions. (Figure 4)

2. Fuse the fast2fuse strip to the wrong side of a 2½" × 26" purse bottom piece.

Buckle

1. Fold the 2¼″ × 15″ cotton print rectangle in half lengthwise with right sides together. Sew a ¼″ seam allowance down the length of the fabric to form a tube.

2. Turn the tube right side out and press with the seam positioned in the center. (Figure 5)

3. Cut the tube into 2 pieces—1 piece 6″ long and another piece 8″ long.

4. Fold the 8″ tube in half with seam sides together to form a 4″ length; press. Slip on the D-ring and sew in place ½″ from the fold. Baste the cut ends together ¼″ from the end. (Figure 6)

5. Fold the 6″ tube in half with seam sides together to form a 3″ length; press. Slip on the swivel hook and its D-ring and sew in place ½″ from the fold. Baste the cut ends together ¼″ from the end.

6. Baste the D-ring strap ends to the bottom at the center of the bag front. Baste the swivel hook strap ends to the uniform fabric, centered at the top of the bag back. (Figure 7)

Exterior and Lining

1. Add a Zipper Pocket (page 109) to one of the lining pieces of the purse following the placement guide on the pattern. The pocket opening should be 7½″ when finished.

2. Find and mark the center of each lining and exterior purse shape and the lower-edge rectangles by folding them in half and making a small clip with your scissors. Do the same with the 2½″ × 26″ strips for the purse bottom.

Figure 5

Figure 6

Bag front

Bag back

Figure 7

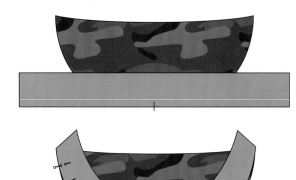
Figure 8

3. Sort the pieces into exterior and lining pieces. The exterior pieces have fast2fuse interfacing applied. Work with one part of the bag at a time, building the exterior first.

4. Match the right side of the purse bottom strip to the front of the purse, aligning the center marks. Ease the strip around the curved shape and pin closely to avoid sewing puckers or folds into the lower edge. Sew the 2 shapes together. *Note: Make sure the D-ring strap is between the bottom and the bag, positioned toward the body of the bag while sewing.* (Figure 8)

5. Repeat Step 4 for the back of the bag.

6. Repeat Step 4 for both lining pieces. The purse lining will be easier to ease around the curve because it has no fused interfacing.

Finishing

1. Turn the purse exterior wrong side out. Place the raw ends of the shoulder strap on the bag exterior and baste them to the right side of the purse. The handle will be tucked inside the purse. (Figure 9)

2. Turn the purse lining right side out and place it into the bag exterior, right sides together. Pin around the upper edge. Sew the exterior and lining together, leaving a 5″ opening at the center back of the purse. Backstitch at the beginning and end of this stitching line. (Figure 10)

3. Turn the bag right side out through the opening. Press flat around the top seamline and press under ½″ at the opening. Pin around the top edge to hold the interfacing in place and hold the seam flat. Edge-stitch (page 102) around the top to finish the bag and close the opening.

Baste here with handles *in* the bag.

Figure 9

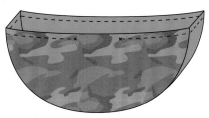
Figure 10

With just enough pockets,
this tote is perfect for books,
crafts, and quick trips.

REVERSIBLE TOTE

★★
★
SKILLED

Finished size: 13″ wide × 13″ high × 3″ deep
Needle: Size 14

Materials and Supplies

1 pair of military uniform pants or
½ yard military-style fabric

1 yard cotton print fabric

⅝ yard 45″-wide dense polyester batting

⅔ yard ⅜″-wide satin or grosgrain ribbon

3″ × 13″ piece of matboard or cardboard

Cutting

TIP Use a 14″ × 14″ freezer-paper template to center and cut the large panel that includes the pocket. Draw this template using an acrylic cutting ruler and a pencil. Press it to the wrong side of the uniform.

UNIFORM FABRIC

- ✪ Cut 1 square 14″ × 14″ centered on large pocket of uniform pants for Side 2.

- ✪ Cut 1 rectangle 9″ × 14″ centered on lower leg pocket or other uniform area for Side 1.

COTTON PRINT FABRIC

- ✪ Cut 2 squares 14″ × 14″ for Sides 1 and 2.

- ✪ Cut 6 strips 4″ × 14″ for sides/bottom.

- ✪ Cut 2 strips 4″ × 24″ for strap.

- ✪ Cut 2 strips 4″ × 14″ for Side 1 (to frame uniform rectangle).

- ✪ Cut 2 strips 3½″ × 13½″ for bag insert.

BATTING

- ✪ Cut 3 strips 4″ × 14″ for sides/bottom.

- ✪ Cut 2 squares 14″ × 14″ for body.

- ✪ Cut 1 strip 4″ × 24″ for strap.

RIBBON

- ✪ Cut 2 pieces 12″ long.

REVERSIBLE TOTE

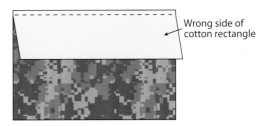

Wrong side of cotton rectangle

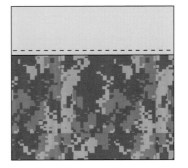

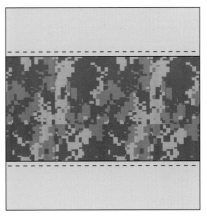

Construction

Seam allowances are ½", unless otherwise noted. Add embellishments, such as nametapes or patches, to areas where they won't interfere with construction of the tote.

Side 1

1. Place the 4" × 14" cotton rectangles on the 9" × 14" uniform rectangle with right sides together. Sew. Press the seam allowances toward the cotton print and edge-stitch (page 102) along the cotton print. Trim this finished panel to 14" × 14" square. You may choose to center the uniform rectangle or have it offset. (Figure 1)

2. Add the side panels to the Side 1 front and back, making sure the pocket is facing up. Place a side panel right sides together on each side of the front of Side 1. Pin and sew, stopping ½" from the bottom. Backstitch at the beginning and end of each seam. Sew the back of Side 1 to the side panels, stopping ½" from the bottom. (Figure 2) *Note: Leave an 8"–10" opening in one of the side seams for turning the bag right side out at the end of construction.*

Figure 1

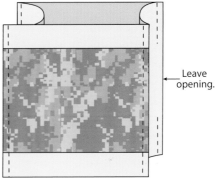

Leave opening.

Figure 2

REVERSIBLE TOTE

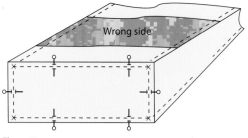

Figure 3

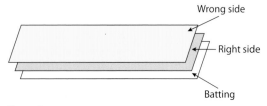

Wrong side

Right side

Batting

Figure 4

Figure 5

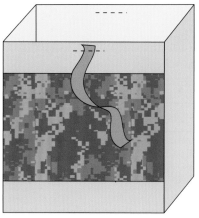

Figure 6

3. To add the bottom panel, pin it in place and sew each side separately, stopping ½" from the corners. This is Y-seam construction. (Figure 3)

Side 2

1. Place all the Side 2 pieces right side up on top of their corresponding batting pieces.

2. Construct Side 2 in the same manner as Side 1; however, Side 2 will be a little more challenging to make because of the batting. Don't leave an opening in any of the side seams.

Strap

1. Layer the 4" × 24" cotton strap pieces right sides together. Place the 4" × 24" piece of batting on the bottom and pin the layers together. (Figure 4)

2. Sew along each 24" side, joining the layers. Backstitch at the beginning and end of each stitching line.

3. Turn the strap right side out, with the right side of each fabric panel on each side. Press. Topstitch ¼" from the edges of the long sides to secure the batting inside the strap. (Figure 5)

Finishing

1. Fold the 14" × 14" Side 1 panels in half to find the center of each top edge. Make a light crease in the fabric and baste the ribbon on the right side of the bag ¼" from the top. (Figure 6)

2. Place the ends of the strap on the right side of the side panels of Side 1. The strap should be the same width as the side panel. Baste the strap in place ¼″ from the top edge. (Figure 7)

3. Turn the Side 1 bag wrong side out. Turn the Side 2 bag right side out.

4. Place the Side 2 bag into the Side 1 bag. Make sure the handles are tucked into the bags. Pin the Side 1 and Side 2 bags together along the top edge, aligning the raw edges and all vertical seam-lines. (Figure 8)

5. Sew around the entire top edge.

6. Carefully turn the bag right side out by pulling the Side 2 bag through the opening in the side seam.

7. Pin the opening closed by turning in the seam allowances and making sure the 2 sides lie smoothly together. Sew the opening closed by hand.

8. Press the top edge of the bag to encourage the batting into a nice flat shape. Topstitch the entire upper edge of the bag.

9. Make a Hard-Bottom Bag Insert (page 105) and place in the bag.

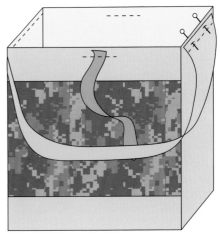

Figure 7

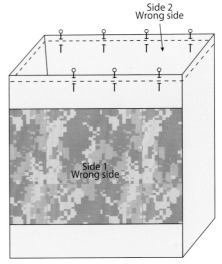

Side 2
Wrong side

Side 1
Wrong side

Figure 8

REVERSIBLE TOTE

CIRCLE PURSE

EXPERIENCED

Scrappy, fresh, trendy, quilted …
what could be better?

Finished size: 11˝ diameter, 3˝ deep
Needles: Size 14 for piecing; size 16 for quilting

Materials and Supplies

Military uniform scraps at least 2″–3½″ × 14″ or 1 fat quarter military-style fabric

½ yard lining fabric

½ yard interior pocket fabric

¼ yard cotton print fabric for purse bottom

15–25 assorted strips 2″–3½″ wide and at least 14″ long*

⅞ yard 20″-wide Shape-Flex fusible interfacing

18″ × 26″ piece of dense ⅛″-thick polyester batting

Water-soluble marker

These strips can be cut from the excess lining, pocket, and bottom fabrics. You will need to piece strips together to make 2 squares each 14″ × 14″.

**Sewing and Quilting
TECHNIQUES**

Quilt Finishing (page 116)

Cutting

Template patterns are on pages 120 and 121. For cutting with freezer-paper templates, see page 14.

COTTON PRINT FABRIC

- Cut 1 strip 4″ × 23″ for purse bottom.
- Cut 4 rectangles using handle facing template.

LINING FABRIC

- Cut 2 circles 12″ in diameter.*
- Cut 1 strip 4″ × 23″ for purse bottom.

POCKET FABRIC

- Cut 2 circles 12″ in diameter.*

SHAPE-FLEX INTERFACING

- Cut 2 circles 12″ in diameter.*
- Cut 4 using handle facing template.
- Cut 1 strip 4″ × 23″ for purse bottom.

BATTING

- Cut 2 circles 12″ in diameter.*
- Cut 1 strip 4″ × 23″ for purse bottom.

* Enlarge the pattern on page 120. Make and use a freezer-paper template (page 14) to accurately cut out the 12″ circles. Or, if you still have old 12″ vinyl records, use one as your cutting template—it's the perfect size!

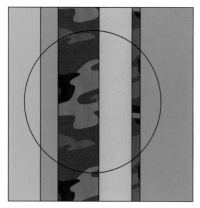

Figure 1

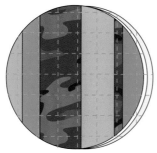

Figure 2

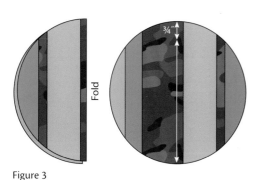

Figure 3

Construction

Seam allowances are ½", unless otherwise noted.

Exterior

1. Sew together the assorted strips of fabric to form 2 squares each measuring at least 14" × 14". Press all the seam allowances in one direction.

2. Cut 2 circles 12" diameter from each pieced square. (Figure 1)

3. Layer a pieced fabric circle, batting circle, and interfacing circle with the batting in the middle. Baste the 3 layers together with pins (page 116). Machine quilt the layers together. Repeat to make a second quilted circle. (Figure 2)

4. Fold each quilted circle in half and press in a crease to mark the center line. Open the pieces. On the right side of each piece, make a mark with a water-soluble marker ¾" down from the top for handle facing placement. Position the fabric strips vertically, as shown in the illustrations, or on an angle, as shown in the photo on page 44. (Figure 3)

CIRCLE PURSE

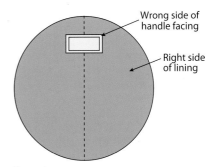
Figure 4

Handles

1. Using the template pattern, mark the center lines and stitching line on the handle interfacing. Fuse the handle interfacing to the wrong side of each fabric handle facing. Make sure you can see your markings on the interfacing.

2. Fold each lining circle in half and press in a crease to mark the center line.

3. Place the handle facings right sides together on the purse exterior and lining circles. Line up the center of all the handle facings with the center crease on each circle so the top edge of the facing is at the ¾" mark. Pin the facing in place on all 4 circles. (Figure 4)

4. Sew on the marked rectangle of the interfacing piece on all 4 circles. (Figure 5)

5. Cut out and remove the center of each sewn rectangle by cutting ¼" *inside* the stitching line. Clip into the corners at an angle, without cutting through the sewing line. Turn the facing to the wrong side by pushing it through the handle opening. Do this for each circle. (Figure 6)

6. Press the handle facing flat against the wrong side of each circle. Use starch to help give the facing a crisp finish. (Figure 7)

7. Use a damp cloth to remove any visible markings from the fabric.

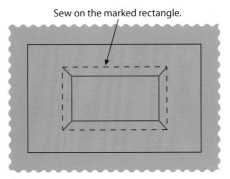
Figure 5

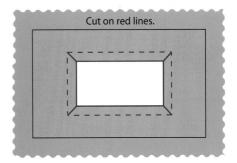
Figure 6

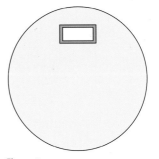
Figure 7

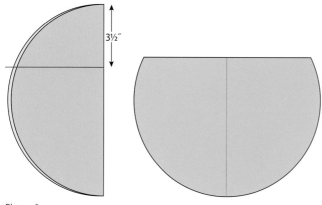

Figure 8

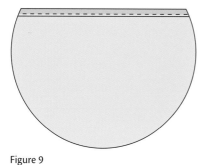

Figure 9

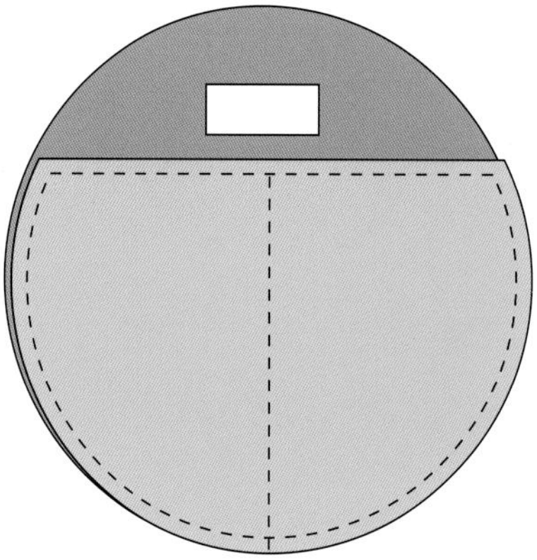

Inside Pockets

1. Fold the pocket circles in half to determine the center lines.

2. Keeping the circles folded, draw lines perpendicular to the folded line and 3½″ down from the top edge. Cut along this line to remove the top portion of the circles. Unfold the circles. (Figure 8)

3. Fold the straight edges ¼″ toward the wrong side twice to create a hem for the top edge of each pocket. Press. Sew these finished folded hem edges a scant ¼″ from the top edge. (Figure 9)

4. Place the pockets wrong side down on the right side of each lining piece, matching the center creased lines and the lower circle edges. Sew along the crease to form 2 pockets, backstitching at the top edge of the pockets. Sew around the lower edge of the circle ⅛″ from the edge to hold the layers in place. (Figure 10)

Figure 10

Purse Sides

1. Place the purse front and lining piece right sides together. Match the circle edges and handle openings. Pin around the perimeter of the circle.

2. Sew around the perimeter with a ⅜″ seam allowance, leaving a 4″ opening along the lower edge. Backstitch at the beginning and end of the sewing line. Sew slowly and carefully to ensure a smooth curved edge. (Figure 11)

3. Repeat Steps 1 and 2 for the purse back. Grade the seam allowances of the circle to reduce bulk (see Tip).

4. Turn the purse front right side out through the 4″ opening along the lower edge. Use a blunt object to push the circle shape out around the edges. Tuck the seam allowances into the opening and sew it closed. Press. Repeat for the purse back.

Finishing the Handles

1. Work with one piece at a time, either the front or the back. Line up the openings of the lining and exterior on each piece. Pin around the opening, holding the layers in place.

2. Hand sew the openings together. Or, for a quicker finish, machine sew around the opening ⅛″ from the edge.

Purse Bottom

1. Layer the cotton print strip, the batting strip, and the interfacing strip for the purse bottom so that the batting is in the middle. Machine quilt the strip as you did for the purse front and back pieces.

2. Place the lining strip right sides together with the quilted strip. Sew around the perimeter, leaving a 4″ opening in the middle of a long side. Backstitch at the starting and stopping points of this stitching line. (Figure 12)

3. Trim the corners from the rectangle to reduce bulk, but don't snip through your stitching lines. Turn the rectangle right side out through the 4″ opening. Press. Sew the opening closed by machine or by hand.

TIP To grade a seam, trim the layers of the seam allowance at varying widths to minimize bulk.

Figure 11

Figure 12

CIRCLE PURSE

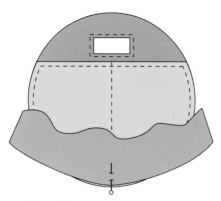

Figure 13

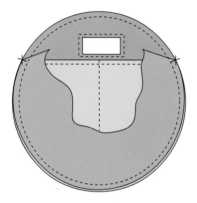

Figure 14

 TIP Sew with the rectangle face up on the sewing machine to make it easer to ease the straight edge of the bottom onto the curved edge of the circle.

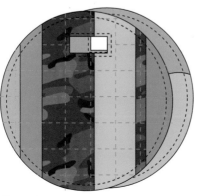

Figure 15

Finishing

1. Fold the purse bottom strip in half and place a pin in the fold to mark the center bottom of the purse.

2. Match the lining side of the circle and the lining side of the rectangle along the bottom, using the pocket stitching as a guide for the center of the purse. Pin around the bottom edge from the lining side of the purse. The purse bottom will end at the top edge of the pocket. (Figure 13)

3. Using the size 16 sewing needle, sew around the circle ¼" from the finished edges. Backstitch securely at the top edge of the rectangle to ensure durability. (Figure 14)

4. Repeat Steps 2 and 3 to attach the other side of the purse. (Figure 15)

CIRCLE PURSE

MILITARY MONSTER TOTE

★
★
★

EXPERIENCED

This extra-large bag is perfect for vacations, for weekends, or as a diaper bag. It has a total of eight drop-in pockets and an interior zippered pocket to keep things secure.

Finished size: 14″ wide x 13½″ high x 7″ deep | **Needle:** Size 16

Sewing and Quilting
TECHNIQUES

Zipper Pocket (page 109)

Center-Applied Zipper
with Lining (page 113)

Bag-Shaping Darts (page 104)

Hard-Bottom Bag Insert (page 105)

Materials and Supplies

1 military uniform shirt or ¾ yard
military-style fabric

1¼ yards print lining fabric

1⅜ yards cotton print fabric

3½ yards 1¼″-wide olive drab cotton webbing

3½ yards ¾″-wide coordinating grosgrain ribbon

22″ plastic nonseparating zipper*

9″ plastic nonseparating zipper

24″ × 64″ piece of dense batting

7″ × 14″ piece of matboard or cardboard

Thread to match ribbon

*You can use the zipper from an army airmen battle
uniform (ABU) shirt if you prefer.*

Cutting

UNIFORM FABRIC

- Cut 2 pieces 10″ × 12″ for exterior pocket.*
- Cut 4 pieces 7″ × 15″ for exterior sides.

LINING FABRIC

- Cut 2 pieces 18″ × 22″ for
  main interior of bag.
- Cut 2 pieces 10″ × 12″ for
  lining of exterior pockets.
- Cut 1 piece 2″ × 12″ for zipper
  facing on welt pocket.
- Cut 1 piece 8″ × 12″ for
  zipper pocket lining.

COTTON PRINT FABRIC

- Cut 4 pieces 8″ × 22″ for interior pockets.
- Cut 2 pieces 10″ × 18″ for large
  center exterior pocket.
- Cut 4 pieces 4″ × 7″ for top corners
  of exterior bag.
- Cut 2 pieces 7½″ × 14½″ for
  Hard-Bottom Bag Insert.

BATTING

- Cut 2 pieces 18″ × 22″ for tote body.
- Cut 2 pieces 7½″ × 22″ for interior pockets.
- Cut 2 pieces 10″ × 12″ for exterior pockets.

WEBBING

- Cut 2 pieces 62″ long.

RIBBON

- Cut 2 pieces 62″ long.

*Make sure there are no heavy uniform seams on the
10″ sides of the pieces.*

Construction

Seam allowances are ½", unless otherwise noted.

Exterior

1. Place the 4" × 7" pieces of cotton print and the 15" × 7" pieces of uniform fabric right sides together. Sew together to make 4 side panels. Press the seam allowances toward the cotton print. Edge-stitch (page 102) this seam for reinforcement. (Figure 1)

2. Make the exterior pockets by layering the 10" × 12" pieces of uniform and lining fabric right sides together. Place the batting on the bottom and pin the layers together. Sew along the top (10") edge.

3. Flip the lining up and around the ½" seam allowance of batting to give the top edge of the pocket a bound look. Press. Stitch in-the-ditch to hold the lining securely on the back of the pocket. (Figure 2) *Note: The lining fabric will be slightly shorter on the inside, and a small amount of batting will be visible. This is fine; it will be enclosed within seams later.*

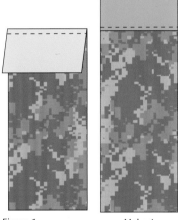

Figure 1   Make 4.

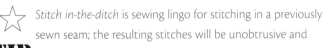

☆ **TIP** *Stitch in-the-ditch* is sewing lingo for stitching in a previously sewn seam; the resulting stitches will be unobtrusive and hardly noticeable.

4. If you plan to add a nametape or patch to the exterior pocket, add it now. It is best placed within 4" of the top edge of the exterior pocket.

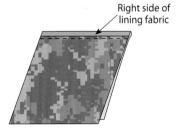

Right side of lining fabric

Figure 2

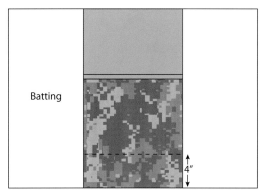

Batting

4″

Figure 3

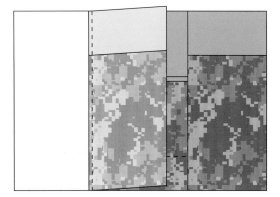

Figure 4

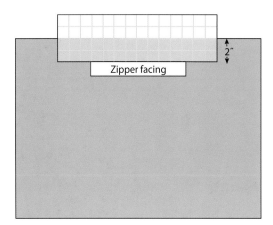

Zipper facing

2″

Figure 5

5. Mark the centers of the 22″ sides of the 18″ × 22″ batting rectangles with a small clip. Mark the centers of the 10″ sides of the 10″ × 18″ cotton print pieces in the same manner. Center the cotton print on the batting, using the clips to align the pieces. Place a pocket piece from Step 3 on each of the cotton print pieces. Align the lower edge of the pocket with the lower edge of the batting rectangle.

6. Pin the pockets and center panels in place. Sew the pockets to the exterior fabric and batting 4″ from the lower edge. This will keep the pockets from being too deep once the bag is finished. (Figure 3)

7. Place the side panels from Step 1 right sides together with the center pocket units. Pin in place and sew through all layers. Press. (Figure 4)

Lining

1. Mark the center of the 22″ side of a lining piece with a clip. Center the top edge of the zipper facing piece 2″ below the top edge of the lining. Make a Zipper Pocket (page 109). (Figure 5)

2. The method for making the lining pockets is the same as for making the exterior pocket unit. For each pocket unit, layer the two 8″ × 22″ cotton print pieces right sides together and place the 7½″ × 22″ batting piece on the bottom. Pin the layers together and sew along one long edge. Flip the top fabric piece to the back side of the pocket unit and stitch in-the-ditch. Trim the fabric even with the lower edge of the batting. (Figure 6)

3. Press both 18″ × 22″ lining pieces. Use a water-soluble pen to mark a line 4″ from the bottom edge along the 22″ length. Place the bottom edge of the lining pocket right sides together on this 4″ line; pin in place. Make sure to fold the zipper pocket lining out of the way. (Figure 7)

4. Sew the pocket to the bag, using the width of the presser foot as the seam allowance. Carefully fold up the pocket and press. Measure and mark 7½″ in from each side edge. Sew perpendicular to the pocket bottom to create pockets, backstitching securely at the top edge of the pockets. (Figure 8)

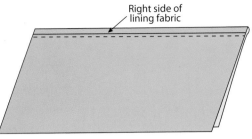

Right side of lining fabric

Figure 6

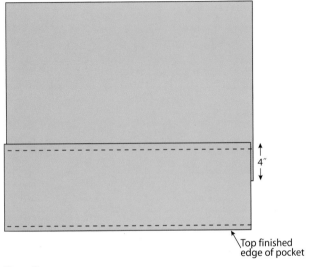

4″

Top finished edge of pocket

Figure 7

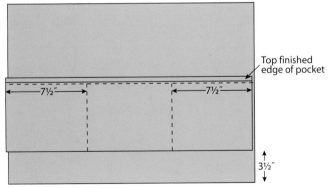

Top finished edge of pocket

7½″   7½″

3½″

Figure 8

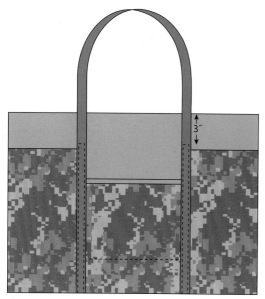

Figure 9

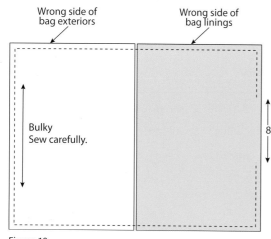

Wrong side of
bag exteriors

Wrong side of
bag linings

Bulky
Sew carefully.

8″

Figure 10

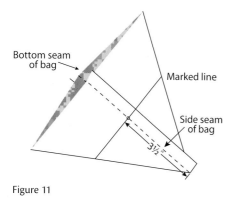

Bottom seam
of bag

Marked line

Side seam
of bag

3½″

Figure 11

Putting It All Together

1. Center the ribbon on the cotton webbing. Edge-stitch along both long edges of the ribbon.

2. Make sure the handles are exactly the same length. Center the handle on one of the vertical seamlines of the bag exterior, matching the cut edge of the handle to the bottom edge of the bag. Edge-stitch the handle to the bag along the right and left sides of the webbing. Stop sewing 3″ from the top edge of the exterior fabric and sew across the handle at the 3″ mark a few times to hold it securely on the bag. This is critical, because the handles will endure much stress and wear during the life of the bag. Sew the other side of the handle in the same manner. (Figure 9)

3. Insert a Center-Applied Zipper with Lining (page 113) and sew the sides together, leaving an 8″–10″ opening. (Figure 10)
Note: If you are using a zipper from an ABU shirt, it will be a couple of inches shorter than the top of the bag. This is perfectly okay. Center the zipper on the top edge of the bag and continue with the Center-Applied Zipper with Lining.

4. Make Bag-Shaping Darts (page 104) in the bag and the lining, using a 3½″ measurement from the point. (Figure 11)

5. Reach inside the lining opening, unzip the zipper completely, and pull the exterior fabric through the zippered opening and out through the opening in the lining. Continue to turn the bag right side out, pushing the darts into place.

6. Sew the opening in the lining closed by hand or machine.

7. Make a Hard-Bottom Bag Insert (page 105).

HOME ✶ FOR THE ✶ HOLIDAYS

PLACEMATS

These placemats are great for honoring your service member who is home or out of town for the holidays. Or replace the holiday print with another novelty print to coordinate with a themed party.

NOVICE

Finished size: 12" x 18" | **Needle:** Size 14

Materials and Supplies

Makes 4 placemats.

1 pair of military uniform pants or shirt or ¾ yard military-style fabric

1⅛ yards cotton holiday print fabric

3 yards decorative trim

¾ yard 45"-wide dense batting or heat-resistant batting, such as Insul-Bright (by The Warm Company)

Cutting

UNIFORM FABRIC

- ❂ Cut 4 squares 12½" × 12½" for placemat centers.*

COTTON PRINT FABRIC

- ❂ Cut 4 rectangles 12½" × 18½" for backing.
- ❂ Cut 8 rectangles 3½" × 12½" for placemat sides.

BATTING

- ❂ Cut 4 rectangles 12½" × 18½".

Although pockets and other decorative unique elements are fun in uniform projects, for these placemats, it is best not to have lumps within your 12½" cut squares. You may need to piece smaller squares or rectangles together to get the size needed.

Construction

Seam allowances are ¼".

1. Place 3½" × 12½" cotton pieces on opposite sides of the uniform fabric square with right sides together; sew. Press the seam allowances toward the narrow rectangles. (Figure 1)

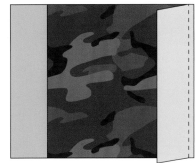

Figure 1

2. Place the decorative trim over the seamlines and sew in place.

3. If you are adding a nametape or other flat embellishment, add it now.

4. Place the pieced placemat top right sides together with the backing rectangle. Add the batting rectangle on the bottom. Sew around the perimeter, leaving a 4" opening along one of the short sides. (Figure 2)

Figure 2

5. Clip the corners at an angle and trim the batting close to the stitching to reduce bulk. Turn the placemat right side out through the opening. Use a blunt object to push out the corners.

6. Sew the opening closed by hand or machine, or secure by edge-stitching (page 102) around all edges.

STOCKING

NOVICE

A fun way to honor service members during the holidays. You can make one for everyone in your family, or fill the stockings and send them to service members who can't make it home for the holidays.

Finished size: approximately 7½″ × 15″ | **Needle:** Size 14

Materials and Supplies

1 military uniform shirt or
1 fat quarter military-style fabric

⅝ yard cotton holiday print lining fabric

½ yard cotton holiday print fabric

8″ piece of ⅜″-wide satin or grosgrain ribbon

Cutting

Template pattern is on page 122. Enlarge the pattern 225%. For cutting with freezer-paper templates, see page 14.

Note ★ *The stocking pieces are asymmetrical, meaning the toe points to the left only. Pay close attention when cutting to ensure that you are cutting 1 back piece and 1 front piece of each from the lining and exterior fabrics.* ★

UNIFORM FABRIC

○ Cut 1 using stocking template.

COTTON PRINT FABRIC

○ Cut 1 using stocking template reversed.

○ Cut 5 strips 2″ × 8½″ for cuff.

○ Cut 2 squares 6″ × 6″ for heel and toe.

LINING FABRIC

○ Cut 1 and 1 reversed using stocking template.

○ Cut 5 strips 2″ × 8½″ for cuff.

○ Cut 2 squares 6″ × 6″ for heel and toe.

Construction

Seam allowances are ½″, unless otherwise noted.

Exterior

1. Fold each edge of the 4 fabric squares ¼″ toward the wrong side. Press. This will conceal the raw edges in the finished project.

2. Arrange the squares to overlap on the heel and toe as desired. Pin the squares in place and edge-stitch around each one. Trim them even with the curve of the stocking heel and toe. (Figure 1)

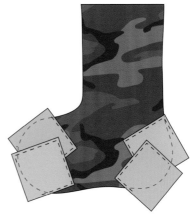

Figure 1

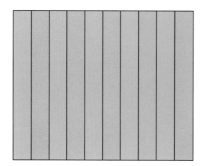

Figure 2

Cuff

1. Sew the 10 fabric strips together using ¼″ seam allowances to form an 8½″ × 15½″ rectangle. Alternate the strip colors as you sew. Press all the seam allowances in one direction. (Figure 2)

2. Sew the 8½″ ends together using a ¼″ seam allowance to form a tube. (Figure 3)

3. Fold the tube in half with wrong sides together to create the cuff for the top of the stocking. Press the fold. (Figure 4)

Figure 3

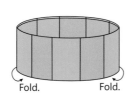

Fold.   Fold.

Figure 4

Exterior and Lining

1. Add any nametape or embellishments to the stocking exterior now.

2. Place the stocking exteriors right sides together. Pin around the perimeter and sew. Repeat for the lining.

3. Make small clips and notches at the curves around the perimeter of the exterior and lining. (Figure 5)

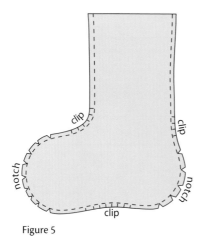

Figure 5

STOCKING

Finishing

1. Make a loop with the ribbon and baste the ends of the ribbon to the right side of the lining on the heel side. (Figure 6)

2. Place the lining into the stocking exterior with wrong sides together. Tuck the ribbon inside the stocking. Place the cuff folded side down into the lining. Pin all 3 units together around the top edge. (Figure 7)

3. Sew around the top of the stocking. Open the cuff and understitch the seam allowances toward the body of the stocking (see Tip below).

  TIP Understitch from the right side of the lining to hold the seam allowance in place toward that side. Sew through the lining and both seam allowances.

4. Fold the cuff to the right side of the stocking to reveal the ribbon loop. Press, hang, and wait for Santa! (Figure 8)

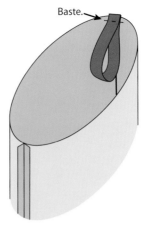

Baste.

Figure 6

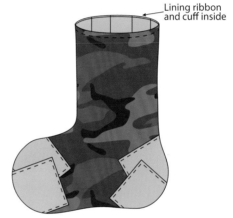

Lining ribbon and cuff inside

Figure 7

Figure 8

TREE SKIRT

Showcase the gifts under the tree with this unique square tree skirt.

Finished size: 40˝ × 40˝ | **Needle:** Size 14

Materials and Supplies

1 military uniform shirt or
⅜ yard military-style fabric

1 fat quarter cotton holiday print
for center

2½ yards cotton holiday print for
outer border and backing

2 yards ⅜″-wide satin or grosgrain ribbon

Cutting

UNIFORM FABRIC

♻ Cut 2 strips 4½″ × 14½″ for middle border.

♻ Cut 2 strips 4½″ × 22½″ for middle border.

COTTON PRINT FAT QUARTER

♻ Cut 1 square 14½″ × 14½″ for center.

COTTON PRINT FABRIC

♻ Cut 2 strips 9½″ × 22½″ for outer border.

♻ Cut 2 strips 9½″ × 40½″ for outer border.

♻ Cut 1 square 40½″ × 40½″ for backing.

RIBBON

♻ Cut 3 pieces 24″ long.

Construction

Seam allowances are ¼″, unless otherwise noted.

Piecing

1. Sew the shorter strips of uniform fabric to the right and left sides of the center square. Press the seam allowances toward the center.

2. Add the remaining uniform strips to the top and bottom of the unit. Press the seam allowances toward the center.

3. Add the shorter outer border strips to the right and left of the uniform fabric pieces, joining the 22½″ sides. Press the seam allowances toward the outer border.

4. Add the remaining outer border strips to the top and bottom edges of the unit. Press toward the outer border. (Figure 1)

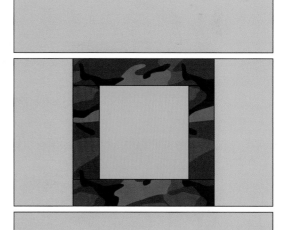

Figure 1

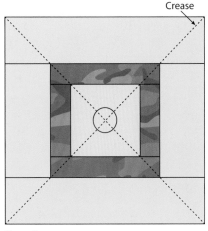

Crease

Figure 2

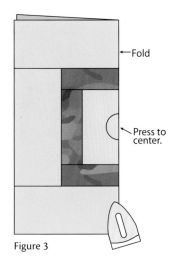

Fold

Press to
center.

Figure 3

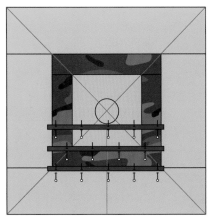

Figure 4

Finishing

1. Fold the tree skirt in half on the diagonal and press lightly at the center. Open it, fold it again on the opposite diagonal, and press lightly in the center. This will locate the exact center of the square unit.

2. Working from the back, mark a 6″ diameter circle centered over the creases. (Figure 2) (Make a template using the pattern on page 120.)

3. Fold the square in half. Press the fold from one edge to the center. This will be your guide for sewing and cutting. (Figure 3)

4. Working from the right side, center a ribbon over the pressed fold at each seamline. Place the third ribbon so that it is ½″ from the edge of the 6″ circle. Pin them in place. You may need to place the 6″ circle template on top of the project to ensure correct ribbon placement. (Figure 4)

5. Place the backing square and the pieced unit right sides together. Pin around the perimeter along the pressed fold and around the marked circle. Make sure the ribbon ends are not within any sewing lines.

6. Sew around the edges of the tree skirt ¼"
away from the fold line and ¼" outside the drawn
circle. Begin on a long exterior side and leave a
6" opening. Backstitch at the beginning and end
of the stitching line. (Figure 5)

7. Cut along the fold guideline and ¼" inside the
circle stitching line. Trim the points from the
corners and clip into the curve of the circle up to,
but not through, the stitching line. (Figure 6)

8. Turn the project right side out through the
opening. Use a blunt object to push the corners
into nice crisp points. Press the edges flat.

9. Tuck the seam allowances into the opening
and pin this opening closed. Edge-stitch
(page 102) around the entire tree skirt.

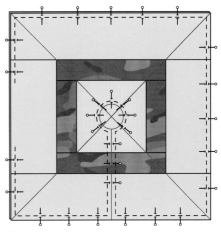

Figure 5

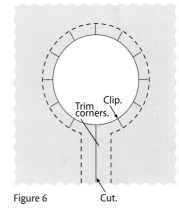

Figure 6

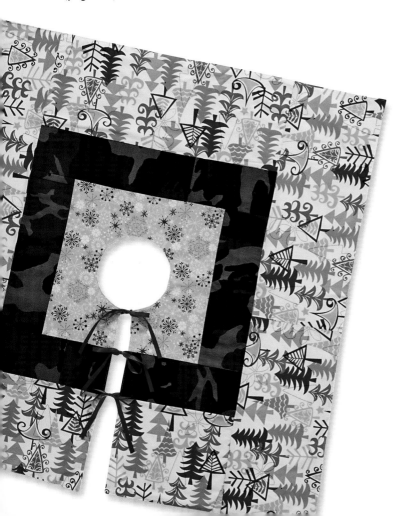

TREE SKIRT

TABLE RUNNER

Finished size: 15″ × 48″
Needle: Size 14

NOVICE

Brighten up the holiday table. If you add insulated batting, you'll have a large functional hot pad for potlucks and festive dinners.

Materials and Supplies

1 military uniform shirt or ⅓ yard military-style fabric

1½ yards cotton holiday print fabric

1 fat quarter cotton holiday print fabric

2 fat eighths cotton holiday print fabric

1½ yards 22″-wide heat-resistant batting,* such as Insul-Bright

*You can use regular batting; however, using a heat-resistant material, such as Insul-Bright or a recycled ironing board cover, will allow the runner to function as a hot pad as well as a table decoration.

Cutting

UNIFORM FABRIC
- Cut 6 strips* 2½″ × 15½″.

COTTON PRINT FABRIC
- Cut 1 rectangle 15½″ × 48½″ for backing.
- Cut 7 strips 3½″ × 15½″.

COTTON PRINT FAT QUARTER
- Cut 5 strips 3½″ × 9½″.

COTTON PRINT FAT EIGHTHS
- Cut 5 squares 3½″ × 3½″ from each.

BATTING
- Cut 1 rectangle 15½″ × 48½″.

*Uniform scraps can be pieced to make the 2½″ × 15½″ strips.

Construction

Seam allowances are ¼″.

1. Place two different 3½″ squares right sides together and sew. Repeat to make a total of 5 pairs.

2. Place the pairs from Step 1 right sides together with the 9½″-long strips and sew to form 5 longer strips.

3. Arrange the pieced strips, the uniform strips, and the holiday print strips, alternating colors, to form the top of the table runner.

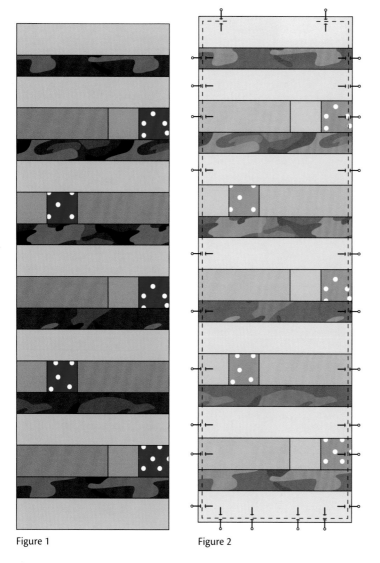

Figure 1

Figure 2

4. Working from top to bottom and keeping the strips in the correct order, place the strips right sides together and sew. Press all the seam allowances in one direction. If you are adding a nametape or any patches, add them after the top is pieced together. (Figure 1)

5. Layer the backing rectangle and the pieced top right sides together. Place the batting on the bottom and pin the layers together.

6. Sew around the edges, leaving a 9″ opening on one short side. (Figure 2)

7. Reduce bulk in the seam allowances by trimming the corners.

8. Turn the table runner right side out. Use a blunt object to push the corners into nice crisp points. Press the edges flat.

9. Tuck the seam allowances into the opening and pin closed. Edge-stitch (page 102) around the perimeter. Quilt the layers together if desired.

TIP You can turn this pieced top into a typical quilted table runner using basic quilting and binding techniques (pages 116–118). You'll need an extra ⅜ yard of fabric for the binding.

QUILTS
* AND *
BABY ITEMS

STROLLER BLANKET

NOVICE

Finished size: 23½″ × 29″ | **Needle:** Size 14

This is the most practical blanket your little one will have. The blanket is narrower than a crib quilt and fits neatly in a stroller. The grommet allows you to attach it to the stroller to keep it from sliding down onto the ground or under the wheels.

Materials and Supplies

1 military uniform shirt or ½ yard military-style fabric

¼ yard each of 2 cotton prints or ½ yard of 1 cotton print

1½ yards 1½"-wide rickrack

Ultrasoft bath towel (approximately 27" × 52") or ¾ yard of Minky fabric, fleece, or other soft fabric for back of blanket

1" metal grommet and grommet tool

Figure 1

Cutting

UNIFORM FABRIC

⚙ Cut 2 strips* 6½" × 30".

COTTON PRINT FABRIC

⚙ Cut 2 strips 6½" × 30".

Piece these from the shirt fabric as needed.

Construction

1. Sew the 4 rectangles together along the long edges with right sides together, using a ¼" seam. Press all the seam allowances in one direction. (Figure 1)

2. Pin the rickrack 6½" from the lower edge of the pieced front and sew in place. Sew the remaining rickrack 2" above the first row of rickrack. Trim the rickrack even with the edges. (Figure 2)

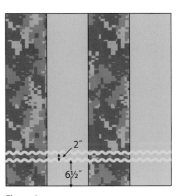

Figure 2

3. Place the pieced front and the towel or fleece right sides together. Pin around all the edges and cut off the excess towel or fleece. Sew around the edges using a ½" seam allowance. Leave a 6" opening along one 30" side and backstitch at the beginning and end of the stitching. Clip the corners of the seam allowance to reduce bulk. (Figure 3)

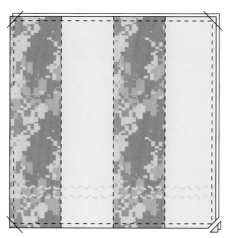

Figure 3

4. Turn the blanket right side out through the opening. Use a blunt object to gently push the corners into a nice square shape. Press. Fold the seam allowance into the opening. Pin in place and edge-stitch (page 102) around the entire blanket.

5. Insert the metal grommet in an upper corner of the blanket, following the manufacturer's directions.

Here's a great baby accessory for when you're on the go or at home. Using the large pant-leg pocket gives you storage space for a couple of diapers and other necessary supplies for the little one.

CHANGING PAD

NOVICE

Finished size: 16˝ × 19˝ | **Needle:** Size 16

Materials and Supplies

1 pair of military uniform cargo pants
or ⅝ yard military-style fabric

⅝ yard cotton print for lining

17″ × 20″ piece of batting*

1″ × 33″ piece of batting*

*This can be batting scraps pieced together from other projects.

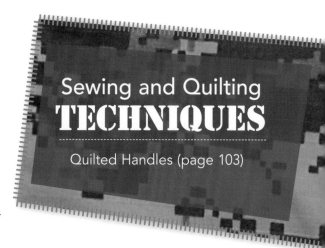

Sewing and Quilting
TECHNIQUES

Quilted Handles (page 103)

Cutting

Note ★ *When preparing the uniform pants, cut the pant leg open, making sure the large cargo pocket is intact. You'll want to cut the rectangle so that you have about 3″ of fabric above the top edge of the pocket. The 17″ side of the rectangle will be along the top of the pocket, and the 20″ sides will be parallel to the pocket sides. ★*

UNIFORM FABRIC

✿ Cut 1 rectangle 17″ × 20″.

COTTON PRINT FABRIC

✿ Cut 1 rectangle 17″ × 20″.

✿ Cut 2 rectangles 3″ × 17″ for handles.

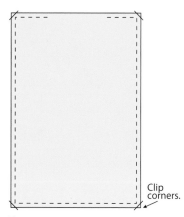

Figure 1

Construction

1. Apply the nametape or any embellishments. Place the nametape, or any patch with writing, on the end opposite the pocket so the names and words will be right side up when the changing pad is rolled. (Figure 1)

2. Layer the uniform fabric and lining fabric rectangles right sides together. Add the batting and pin. Sew around the rectangles with a ½″ seam allowance, leaving an 8″ opening along one short side. Backstitch at the beginning and end of the stitching. Clip the corners to reduce bulk. (Figure 2)

Clip corners.

Figure 2

3. Turn the changing pad right side out through the opening. Use a blunt object to push the corners into a nice square shape. Tuck the seam allowances into the opening, pin, and edge-stitch (page 102) around the rectangle.

4. Measure and mark 2 quilting lines 3″ from the long sides. If the 3″ line intersects the pocket, adjust it by moving it closer to the finished edge. (Figure 3)

5. Join the short ends of the two 3″ × 17″ handle rectangles, using a ¼″ seam allowance, to make one long strip. Press the seam allowances to one side and make a Quilted Handle (page 103). Make the long quilted handle into a loop, folding one end toward the seam side and overlapping it with the other end of the handle by 1″. Pin the ends together at the overlap and sew together. (Figure 4)

6. Divide the handle loop into 4 equal sections by folding it in half twice, using the overlapped end as a halfway point. Mark each division with a pin.

7. Position the looped handle on the exterior of the changing pad so that the overlap and the opposite pin are 3″ from the finished edge of the changing pad. Place the folded side of the overlap on the top to conceal the cut ends. The interior edges of the handles should be 2½″ from the center of the changing pad.

8. You will sew along the quilted lines of the handle to attach it to the changing pad. Begin at the edge of the changing pad; backstitch and sew for 6″. Pivot and sew across the handle to the outer quilted stitching line. Pivot and sew 6″ back to the edge; pivot to sew across the handle and backstitch where you began stitching. You'll be sewing a 6″-long rectangle. Repeat for the other side of the handle. (Figure 5)

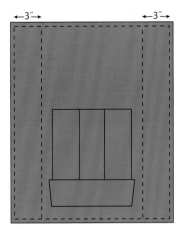

Figure 3

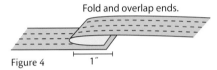

Fold and overlap ends.

Figure 4   1″

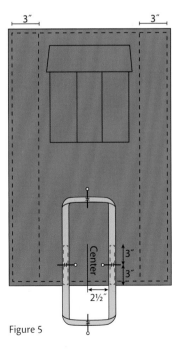

Figure 5

TRIANGLE JUBILEE

★ ★ ★

EXPERIENCED

Finished size: 48˝ × 48˝
Needles: Size 14 for piecing; size 16 for quilting

The perfect size to cozy up on the couch with and help you feel close to your service members, even while they're deployed.

Materials and Supplies

1 military uniform shirt and pair of pants in dark camouflage* or 1⅛ yards military-style fabric

⅝ yard each of 3 light cotton prints or 2 yards total of assorted light scraps

½ yard each of 2 dark cotton prints or 1 yard total of assorted dark scraps

½ yard light print cotton for binding

3 yards cotton fabric for backing

54″ × 54″ piece of low-loft cotton quilt batting

The dark camouflage is best for this quilt; however, I used the lighter camouflage print for the small 2″ squares of the Four-Patch units. You can use either uniform fabric for those 2″ squares.

Cutting

UNIFORM FABRIC

- ✪ Cut 20 squares 7″ × 7″; cut 5 in half diagonally to yield 10 triangles.
- ✪ Cut 20 squares 2″ × 2″.

1 LIGHT PRINT

- ✪ Cut 6 squares 7″ × 7″.
- ✪ Cut 10 squares 3⅞″ × 3⅞″; cut in half diagonally to yield 20 triangles.
- ✪ Cut 20 squares 2″ × 2″.

2 LIGHT PRINTS

- ✪ Cut a total of 21 squares 7″ × 7″.

DARK PRINTS

- ✪ Cut 12 squares 7″ × 7″ (6 from each).

BINDING FABRIC

- ✪ Cut 6 strips 2½″ × width of fabric.

Construction

Seam allowances are ¼".

Blocks

1. Make 10 Four-Patch units using the 2" uniform squares and light-color cotton squares by placing the squares right sides together and sewing. Press the finished units. (Figure 1)

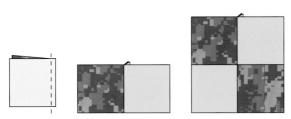

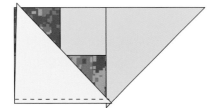

Figure 1

2. Align a small matching light triangle with one side of each Four-Patch unit, right sides together, and sew. Add a second triangle to the adjacent side and sew. Press the finished units. (Figure 2)

Note: The uniform fabric pieces are treated as darks and will be referred to as darks along with the dark cotton prints.

Figure 2

3. Select any 5 dark fabric 7" squares and cut them in half diagonally to make 10 triangles. (The quilt shown uses all uniform fabrics for these.)

4. Place the triangle units created in Step 2 and the dark triangles right sides together. The dark triangles are cut just a bit oversized. Center the edge of the pieced units on the triangle. Sew along the diagonal edge. Be careful not to stretch or pull this edge as you sew. Press the seam allowances toward the darker fabric. (Figure 3)

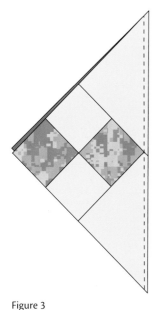

Figure 3

5. Trim and square up the blocks to 6½″ × 6½″. Make 10. (Figure 4)

6. Fold a diagonal line on the light 7″ squares. Place each square right sides together with a dark 7″ square; sew ¼″ on each side of the fold line.

7. Cut along the diagonal line to yield 2 half-square triangle blocks per pair. Press the blocks and trim to 6½″ × 6½″. Make 54. (Figure 5)

Assembly

1. Arrange the blocks in 8 rows of 8 blocks each. This quilt design is based on the contrast created by the light and dark fabrics. Feel free to arrange the quilt top in any pleasing fashion.

2. After the blocks are arranged, place them right sides together and sew them into rows. Press the seam allowances for each row in alternate directions so the seams will nest when you sew the rows together.

3. Pin the rows together, aligning the seams, and sew. After all the rows are sewn together, press all the seam allowances down. (Figure 6)

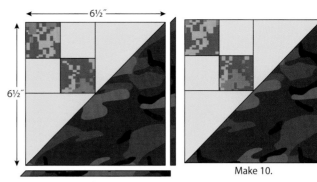

Make 10.

Figure 4

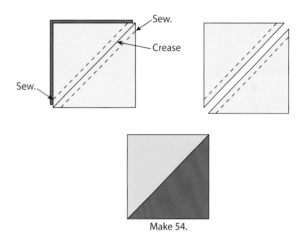

Sew.

Crease

Sew.

Make 54.

Figure 5

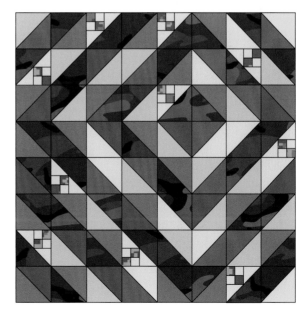

Figure 6

Triangle Jubilee **81**

Finishing

1. Cut the backing fabric in half to make 2 pieces approximately 40″ × 54″. Sew the long sides together and trim to make a backing that is approximately 54″ × 54″.

2. Layer the quilt top, batting, and backing. Baste and quilt as desired (page 116). Finish the quilt with binding (page 117).

SENSATIONAL STRIPS

This easy, quick quilt
makes a wonderful gift
for a new baby.

Finished size: approximately 58″ × 50″
Needles: Size 14 for piecing; size 16 for quilting

NOVICE

Construction

Seam allowances are ¼".

Materials and Supplies

1 military uniform shirt and pair of pants or ¾ yard military-style fabric

10 fat quarters cotton print fabrics

½ yard cotton print for binding

3⅛ yards cotton fabric for backing

64" × 56" piece of batting

Cutting

UNIFORM FABRIC

✿ Cut 12 strips 3" × 20".

✿ Cut 4 strips 3" × 10".

COTTON PRINT
FAT QUARTERS

✿ Cut 41 strips 3" × 20".

✿ Cut 10 strips 3" × 10".

BINDING FABRIC

✿ Cut 6 strips 2½" × width of fabric.

Quilt Top

When piecing, keep in mind that this quilt is designed to be random and scrappy looking.

1. Place a pair of the 3" × 20" strips right sides together; sew to make a partial row. Make 20. (Figure 1)

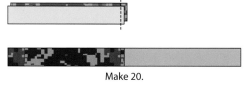

Make 20.

Figure 1

2. Sew an additional 3" × 20" strip to one end of 13 of the rows from Step 1. Sew a 3" × 10" strip to each end of the remaining 7 rows. Press the seam allowances in all 20 rows in one direction. (Figure 2)

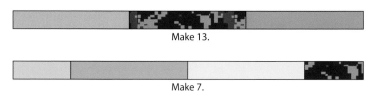

Make 13.

Make 7.

Figure 2

3. Arrange the 20 rows on a work surface, floor, or design wall. To keep the scrappy look, try to make sure that no similar fabrics touch. When you are pleased with the layout, number the rows so they do not become mixed up when you carry them to your sewing machine.

4. Fold and mark the center of each row. Place the rows right sides together, match the centers, and sew the rows together. You may need to re-press some of the seam allowances so that they will be pressed in opposite directions when sewing.

5. Use a rotary cutter and ruler to trim the uneven edges.

Finishing

1. Cut the backing fabric in half to make 2 pieces approximately 40″ × 56″. Sew the long sides together and trim to make a backing that is at least 64″ × 56″.

2. Layer the quilt top, batting, and backing. Baste and quilt as desired (page 116). Finish the quilt with binding (page 117).

· ACCESSORIES ·

Note cards are a great way to ease into sewing without making a large project. Simple, handmade cards come from the heart and, in this case, use up lots of fabric scraps. The most fun feature is that no two cards will be exactly the same. This particular project is wonderfully simple, and even children can help make the cards.

Finished size: 4¼˝ × 5½˝ | **Needle:** Size 14

★

NOVICE

Materials and Supplies

Assorted military uniform scraps or scraps of military-style fabric

Assorted bright cotton scraps

Gluestick

5½" × 8½" piece of cardstock

4" × 5¼" piece of coordinating cardstock to match one of the fabric scraps

Clear tape

Decorative threads (*optional*)

> **Note** ★ *If you want to make several cards, purchase a package of cardstock paper in one color or assorted colors. You can purchase standard card-size envelopes from most discount and office supply stores.* ★

Cutting

Cut at least 4–5 rectangles (or other shapes) about 1" × 2" from a variety of fabrics. The size can vary up to an inch in either direction. These pieces do not need to be a nice square cut, so you can cut them with your scissors in loose, free-form shapes.

Construction

1. Fold the 5½" × 8½" piece of cardstock in half and place the cut fabric pieces so they overlap one another on the front of the card. (Figure 1)

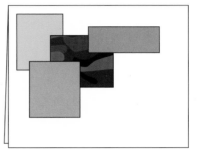

Figure 1

2. Use a gluestick to temporarily hold each piece of fabric in place.

3. Unfold the card. Using a longer-than-normal stitch length, sew long straight lines over the card's entire front surface. The stitching is decorative and will also secure the fabric rectangles in place. Feel free to be creative with the stitching and threads. Leave long thread tails at the beginning and end. (Figure 2)

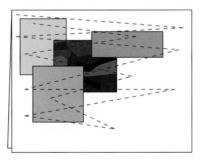

Figure 2

4. Pull the thread ends to the inside of the card. Place a small piece of tape over the ends.

5. Glue the coordinating cardstock to the interior of the card to cover the stitching.

DRINK COASTERS

Coordinate your tabletop with the seasons by whipping up these quick drink coasters. They also make a fun hostess gift.

Finished size: 4″ × 4″ | **Needle:** Size 14

NOVICE

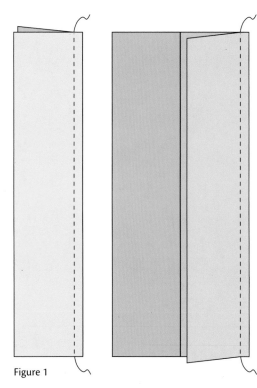

Figure 1

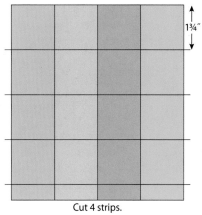

1¾"

Cut 4 strips.

Figure 2

Materials and Supplies

Makes 4 coasters. This project can be made from fabric scraps or charm squares (precut 5" squares of fabric).

1 military uniform shirt or scraps of military-style fabric

4 squares of fabric 5" × 5" each for backing

1 cotton print fat eighth or 4 scraps measuring 2" × 8"

4 batting scraps 5" × 5" each

Cutting

UNIFORM FABRIC

- ✿ Cut 4 strips 2½" × 5" for coaster fronts.

- ✿ Cut 4 strips 1¾" × 5" for coaster fronts.

COTTON PRINT OR SCRAPS

- ✿ Cut 4 strips 1¾" × 8" for coaster fronts.

Construction

Seam allowances are ¼", unless otherwise noted.

Accent Strip

1. Place 2 cotton print 1¾" × 8" strips right sides together and sew. Add the remaining 2 strips. Press the seam allowances in one direction. (Figure 1)

2. Cut the strip-pieced unit into 4 accent strips each 1¾" wide. Trim each to 5" long. (Figure 2)

3. Piece together a narrow uniform strip, an accent strip, and the wider uniform strip. Edge-stitch (page 102) the pieced strip. (Figure 3)

4. Layer the pieced coaster and a 5″ backing square with right sides together. Add a batting square. Pin to hold the layers together.

5. Sew around the coaster with a ½″ seam allowance, leaving a 2″ opening along one nonseamed side. Backstitch at the beginning and end of the sewing line.

6. Clip the corners of the seam allowance to reduce bulk after the coaster is turned right side out. Cut the batting as close to the stitching as possible. (Figure 4)

7. Turn the coaster right side out through the 2″ opening. Use a blunt object to gently push the corners into a nice square shape. Press.

8. Sew the opening closed by edge-stitching all around the coaster.

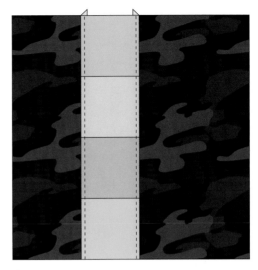

Figure 3

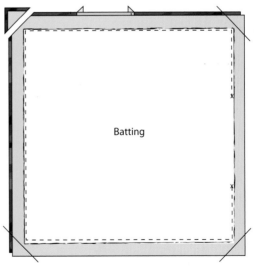

Batting

Figure 4

DRINK COASTERS

BUSINESS CARD HOLDER

NOVICE

Show that your business supports our troops by showcasing your cards in this card holder.

Finished size: 4″ × 2¾″ | **Needle:** Size 14

Materials and Cutting

UNIFORM OR
EQUIVALENT MILITARY-STYLE FABRIC

- Cut 1 rectangle 4½″ × 7¼″ for exterior.
- Cut 1 rectangle 4½″ × 7¼″ for lining.

OTHER SUPPLIES

- Cut 2½″ piece of ¼″-wide grosgrain ribbon.
- Select ¾″-diameter button or cut button off uniform.
- Select coordinating embroidery floss.

Figure 1

Construction

1. Fold the ribbon in half. Choose the fabric that you want for the exterior and baste the ribbon to the right side at the center of one short edge, making sure the ends of the ribbon are even with the edge of the fabric. (Figure 1) *Note: I used the military fabric for the exterior fabric, but you can use either fabric.*

2. Place the rectangles right sides together and sew a scant ¼″ seam allowance around the perimeter, leaving a 2″ opening to turn the card holder right side out. Trim the excess fabric from the corners. (Figure 2)

3. Turn the card holder right side out. Use a blunt object to push the corners to a nice crisp shape.

4. Fold the seam allowances into the opening and pin it closed. Press the unit flat. Do not sew the opening closed yet.

5. Fold the short edge of the finished rectangle up 2½″ and pin it in place. Begin at the lower right edge and sew up the side, across the top, and down the other side ⅛″ from the edges. Backstitch at the beginning and end of your edge stitching (page 102). The edge stitching will close the pinned opening. (Figure 3)

6. Sew the button in place using coordinating embroidery floss.

Figure 2

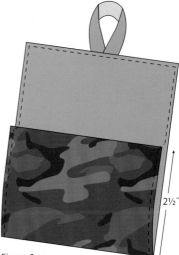

2½″

Figure 3

CHECKBOOK COVER

NOVICE

This is a great small project for scraps. It's very quick to make and is a wonderful gift item.

Finished size: 3½″ × 6½″ | **Needle:** Size 14

Materials and Cutting

UNIFORM OR
EQUIVALENT MILITARY-STYLE FABRIC

- Cut 1 strip 1½″ × 13″ for exterior.

- Cut 1 rectangle 4¾″ × 13″ for exterior.

COTTON PRINT FABRIC

- Cut 1 strip 1¾″ × 13″ for accent strip.

- Cut 1 rectangle 7″ × 13″ for lining.

Construction

Seam allowances are ¼″.

1. Place the 1½″ × 13″ uniform strip and the
1¾″ × 13″ cotton print strip right sides together;
sew. Press the seam allowances toward the
cotton print. (Figure 1)

2. Place the remaining uniform piece right sides
together with the cotton print side of the unit
created in Step 1; sew. Press the seam allowances
toward the cotton print. (Figure 2)

3. Place the lining piece and the unit created in
Step 2 right sides together. Pin and sew around
the outside edge, leaving a 3″ opening on one
side. Backstitch at the starting and stopping
points. (Figure 3)

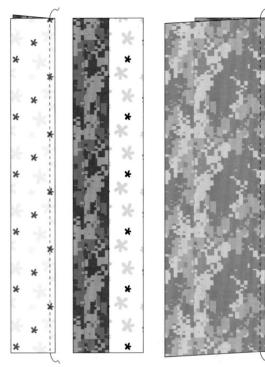

Figure 1   Figure 2

Figure 3

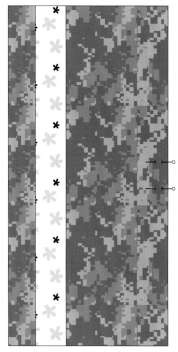

Figure 4

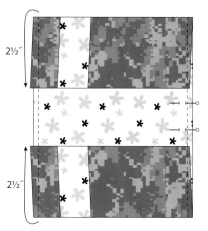

2½″

2½″

Figure 5

4. Clip the corners to reduce bulk. Turn the cover right side out through the opening. Use a blunt object to gently push the corners into a nice square shape. Press.

5. Fold the seam allowances into the opening. Pin in place. (Figure 4)

6. Fold each short end 2½″ toward the lining center. Edge-stitch (page 102) down the right and left sides. (Figure 5)

PASSPORT COVER

Another easy scrap project to dress up your most important travel accessory. This passport cover is designed to fit a standard U.S. passport.

Finished size: 3¾″ × 5½″ | **Needle:** Size 14

Materials and Cutting

UNIFORM OR EQUIVALENT MILITARY-STYLE FABRIC

○ Cut 1 rectangle 4" × 6" for exterior.

COTTON PRINT FABRIC

○ Cut 1 rectangle 6" × 11" for lining.

○ Cut 2 rectangles 4" × 6" for exterior.

⅜"-WIDE SATIN OR GROSGRAIN RIBBON

○ Cut 2 pieces 8" long.

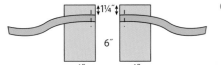
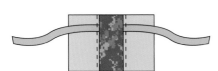

Figure 1

Construction

Seam allowances are ¼".

1. Place a cut ribbon 1¼" from the top of each exterior cotton print rectangle, aligning the raw edges. Baste the ribbons in place. (Figure 1)

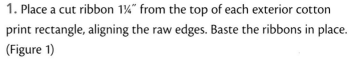

Figure 2

2. With right sides together, sew the cotton prints to the sides of the uniform rectangle. Press the seam allowances toward the cotton print. Edge-stitch (page 102) along the cotton print and through the ribbon. (Figure 2)

3. Place the lining and pieced exterior right sides together. Tuck in the ribbon so the ends don't get caught in the stitching line. Pin and then sew, leaving a 3" opening on one long side. Backstitch at the starting and stopping points. (Figure 3)

Figure 3

4. Clip the corners to reduce bulk. Turn the cover right side out through the opening. Use a blunt object to gently push the corners into a nice square shape. Press.

5. Fold the seam allowances into the opening. Pin in place. Press.

6. Fold each short end 1½" toward the center and pin. Edge-stitch along the top and bottom of the project. This edge stitching will also close the opening on the side of your passport cover. (Figure 4)

7. Fold the cover in half and check that the ribbon ends line up; press.

8. Insert the passport and tie the ribbons in a bow or knot.

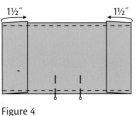

Figure 4

PASSPORT COVER

This is a great pillow to snuggle up with and will serve as a reminder of your family member at home or away.

SKILLED

Finished size: 18″ × 18″ | **Needle:** Size 14

Materials and Supplies

1 military uniform shirt or
½ yard military-style fabric

⅔ yard cotton print fabric or
home decorator–weight fabric

16″ plastic nonseparating zipper*

18″ × 18″ pillow form

Freezer paper

You may also use the zipper from the front of the uniform shirt.

Sewing and Quilting
TECHNIQUES

Center-Applied Zipper (page 111)

Cutting

See Making the Template (below).

UNIFORM FABRIC

✪ Cut 2 triangles using
freezer-paper template.

COTTON PRINT FABRIC

✪ Cut 2 triangles using
freezer-paper template.

✪ Cut 1 square 18½″ × 18½″ for pillow back.

Making the Template

Make a template by drawing a right triangle on the paper (dull) side of freezer paper; the short sides should each be 14″ long. Draw the arrow and place it on the straight of grain (page 102).

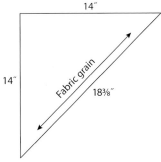

14″

14″

Fabric grain

18⅜″

ACCENT PILLOW

Construction

Seam allowances are ½".

Note: Two edges of the fabric triangles are cut on a bias (45° angle). Be careful not to stretch these edges as you sew.

1. Place the uniform fabric triangles and cotton print triangles right sides together and sew along one of the bias edges. Press the seam allowances toward the cotton. (Figure 1)

2. Place the joined triangle pieces right sides together and sew, making sure the seamlines at the center of the pillow front are aligned. Press the seam allowances to one side. (Figure 2)

3. Insert a Center-Applied Zipper (page 111), using the pillow back and the pieced pillow front.

4. Place the pillow front and the pillow back right sides together. Open the zipper slightly and sew around the remaining 3 sides of the pillow.

5. Clip the corners to reduce bulk and turn the pillow right side out through the open zipper. Use a blunt object to push the corners into a nice crisp shape. Press.

6. Insert the 18″ × 18″ pillow form.

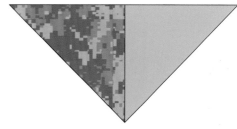

Figure 1

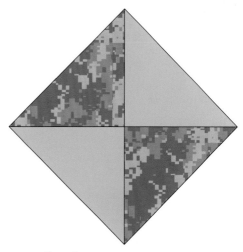

Figure 2

SEWING AND QUILTING TECHNIQUES

✪ Grainlines ✪

The suggested fabrics for projects in this book are woven cotton fabrics and are generally cut on the straight of grain, lengthwise or crosswise.

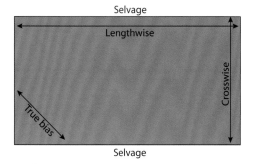

✪ Edge Stitching ✪

Edge stitching is a visible sewing line ⅛″ away from an edge or seamline. It can be decorative or functional (for example, closing openings that are left open to turn an item right side out).

✪ Quilted Handles ✪

Quilted bag handles are an alternative to traditional prefabricated bag handles. These are soft to hold and durable through daily use. Make these handles from fabric that matches or coordinates with the item you are making; for a scrappy, eclectic look, consider piecing a variety of fabrics together to create the 3″ fabric strip. Quilted handles can be used in place of cotton or nylon webbing handles in various projects throughout this book.

Supplies for 1 handle

Fabric: 1 strip 3″ wide, cut to needed length

Dense batting: 1 strip 1″ wide, cut to needed length

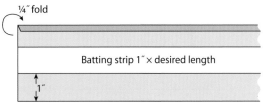

¼″ fold

Batting strip 1″ × desired length

1″

1. Press a ¼″ fold toward the wrong side along the entire length of the 3″-wide strip on one edge. Place the 1″-wide batting strip on the wrong side of the fabric strip, 1″ from the unfolded raw edge.

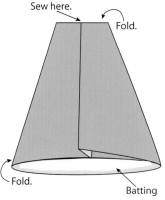

Sew here.

Fold.

Fold.

Batting

2. Fold the unpressed edge over to cover the batting strip. Fold the pressed edge over the batting and fabric. Pin in place and sew next to the center fold the entire length of the strap.

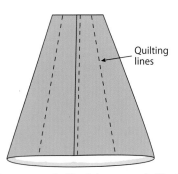

Quilting lines

3. Sew ¼″ away on each side of the center stitching line. The handle is quilted and ready to sew into your project as directed.

SEWING AND QUILTING TECHNIQUES

✪ Bag-Shaping Darts ✪

These easy darts will give a square shape at the sides and a flat bottom to any bag. The distance that you sew along the side seam determines the width of the sides and bottom of the bag. The longer the distance, the wider (and shorter) the bag will be.

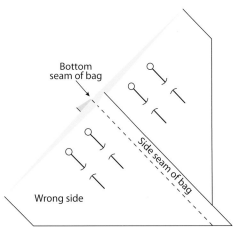

1. With the bag exterior (or lining) wrong side out, fold the bottom of the bag so the side seam lines up with the bottom seam to form a triangle shape. The seams should be finger-pressed in opposite directions so that they nest when you form the triangle shape. Pin to hold the layers together.

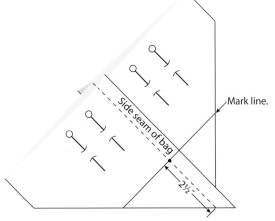

2. Measure the specified distance along the side seam (2½" in the illustration). Make a dot and draw a line perpendicular to the stitching line. This is the sewing line for the dart.

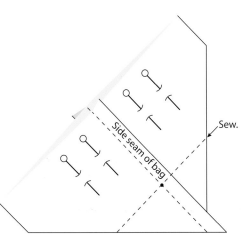

3. Sew directly on the marked line, backstitching at the beginning and end.

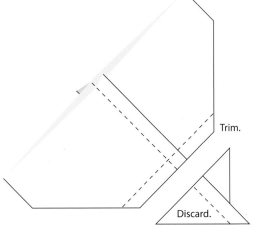

4. Cut off the excess triangle fabric at least ¼" away from your stitching line. Discard the corner.

5. Repeat Steps 1–4 for the other side of the bag.

✪ Hard-Bottom ✪ Bag Insert

A stiff insert in the bottom of any bag will help the bag maintain its shape when filled with all sorts of goodies. Covering it with fabric ensures that it will look great and not be a design distraction in your beautiful project. You can purchase scrap matboard or even pick up matboard scraps for free at your local frame shop. If matboard isn't available, consider gluing a couple of layers of cereal boxes together to achieve the strength of matboard.

Supplies for 1 insert

Matboard: 1 piece, cut to bottom interior dimensions

Lining fabric: 2 rectangles, ½″ bigger than matboard

Leave open.

Fold in ¼″ and stitch.

1. Place the fabric rectangles right sides together, pin, and sew a scant ¼″ seam allowance around 3 sides, leaving a short side unstitched.

2. Turn the piece right side out. Slide in the matboard.

3. Fold the remaining seam allowances into the opening. Edge-stitch the opening closed or, if you prefer, sew by hand.

4. Place the insert into the bottom of the bag.

✪ Welt Pocket ✪

A welt pocket is an excellent pocket option when you want to add a small amount of contrasting color to a design or make a pocket where only the opening shows. The Zipper Pocket (page 109) is similar but more secure. You can use this technique for any garment or accessory. Adjust the sizes as needed—the pocket placement marking is a rectangle ¾″ tall and usually 2″ shorter than the pocket facing.

Supplies for 4″ pocket

Lining fabric:

1 rectangle 4½″ × 5″ for pocket flap

1 rectangle 2″ × 6″ for pocket facing

1 rectangle 6″ × 10″ for pocket lining

Shape-Flex fusible interfacing:

1 rectangle 2″ × 6″ for pocket facing

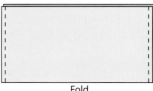

Fold

1. Make the pocket flap by folding the 4½″ × 5″ rectangle in half with right sides together, matching the 4½″ right sides. Using a ¼″ seam allowance, sew the right and left sides. Turn the flap right side out and press.

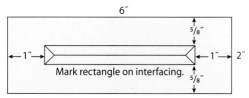

Mark rectangle on interfacing.

2. Fuse the Shape-Flex fusible interfacing to the wrong side of the pocket facing and draw a rectangle ¾″ × 4″ centered in both directions. Draw a line in the center, ending ¼″ from each end. Draw diagonal lines to each corner at a 45° angle. This will be your cutting line later.

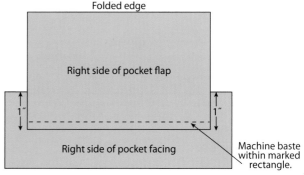

Folded edge

Right side of pocket flap

Right side of pocket facing

Machine baste within marked rectangle.

3. Baste the pocket flap to the right side of the pocket facing, matching the cut edge of the flap with the center line and 1″ down from the edge of the pocket facing. Hold the flap and facing up to the light to ensure proper placement within the marked rectangle guidelines. The wrong side of the pocket flap should touch the right side of the facing.

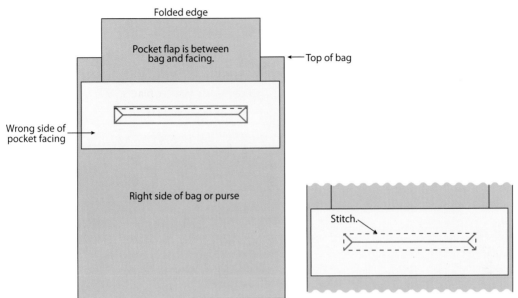

Folded edge

Pocket flap is between
bag and facing.

← Top of bag

Wrong side of
pocket facing →

Right side of bag or purse

4. Place the facing rectangle on the predetermined pocket area of the bag or purse. Match the right side of the item to the right side of the facing. The pocket flap will be pointing up, out of the way.

Stitch.

5. Sew along the marked rectangle over the open end of the pocket flap. At each corner, lower the needle into the fabric, lift the presser foot, and pivot the fabric 90° for a crisp corner. *Note: The sides of the pocket flap should be very near, but not caught in, the stitching at the short ends of the rectangle.*

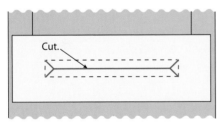

Cut.

6. Cut along the center marked line and snip the diagonal lines toward the corners. Do *not* snip through the pocket stitching lines. Snipping through the basting stitches is okay.

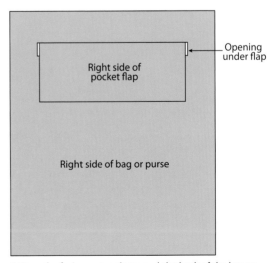

Right side of
pocket flap

Opening
under flap

Right side of bag or purse

7. Turn the facing rectangle toward the back of the bag or lining by pushing it through the opening. This will allow the pocket flap to point down, covering the opening. Press.

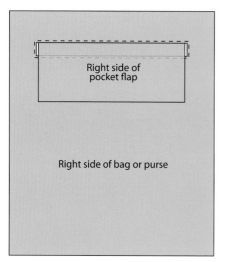

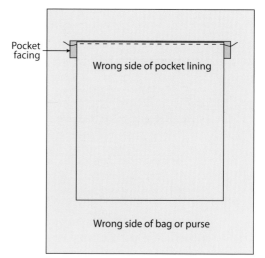

8. Beginning under the pocket flap, sew around the opening from the right side to secure the facing to the wrong side of the project. Do not sew the pocket flap closed.

9. Working from the back, place the 6″ length of the pocket lining on top of the pocket facing, centering it with right sides together. Fold the bag or lining out of the way and sew, using a ¼″ seam allowance and making sure the pocket facing piece is on top.

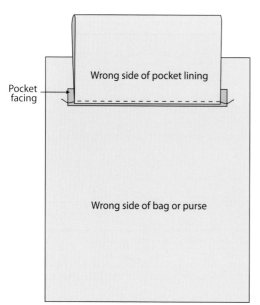

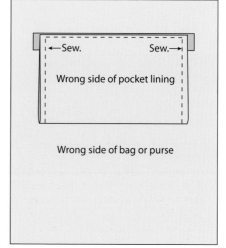

10. Match the lower edge of the pocket lining with the lower edge of the pocket facing, right sides together. Fold the bag or lining out of the way and sew, using a ¼″ seam allowance and with the pocket facing piece on top.

11. Lay the pocket lining piece flat behind the bag or lining in the way it will naturally lie inside the finished bag. Press. Fold the bag or lining out of the way and sew the right and left sides of the pocket lining with a ½″ seam allowance.

✪ Zipper Pocket ✪

The zipper pocket is a wonderful way to add a pocket to your design without altering the integrity of the bag shape or overall design. The zipper pocket is generally used on the bag's interior. The following are general directions for a pocket with a 9″ zipper. If the design needs a zipper opening other than 9″, adjust the measurements on the facing and lining as directed in the specific project instructions. I always use a zipper slightly longer than the desired pocket opening.

Supplies for 1 pocket

Lining fabric:

> 1 strip 2″ × 10″ for pocket facing
>
> 1 rectangle 8″ × 10″ for pocket lining

Zipper: 1 plastic nonseparating, standard 9″-long, and a zipper foot for sewing machine

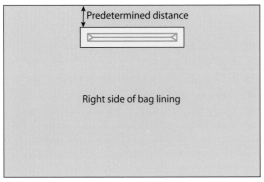

1. Mark a ¾″ × 9″ rectangle in the center on the wrong side of the zipper facing. Draw a line in the center, stopping ¼″ from the ends; then draw diagonal lines to each corner. With right sides together, place the facing rectangle on the lining piece the distance from the top edge indicated in the project you are making.

2. Sew around the marked rectangle; at each corner, lower the needle into the fabric, lift the presser foot, and pivot the fabric 90° for a crisp corner.

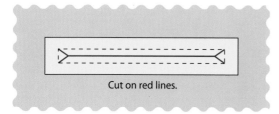

Cut on red lines.

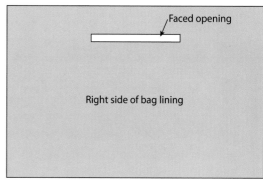

Faced opening

Right side of bag lining

3. Cut along the center marked line and snip the triangle shapes toward the corners. Be careful *not* to snip through the stitching lines.

4. Turn the facing rectangle toward the back of the lining by pushing it through the opening you just cut in Step 3. Press.

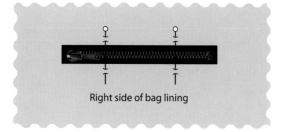

Right side of bag lining

5. Center the zipper behind the newly faced rectangle in the lining. Pin it in place from the front.

6. Place a zipper foot on your machine and position the lining wrong side up. Sew around the facing ⅛" from the edge, sewing through the lining, facing, and zipper tape. Pivot at the corners. *Note: Pay close attention to the zipper. You can sew over plastic zipper teeth, but you can't sew over the metal stopper at the end or top of the zipper. Test the zipper to make sure it opens and closes smoothly.*

7. Follow Steps 9–11 of the Welt Pocket (page 108) to complete a Zipper Welt Pocket. Depending on the project, you may need to trim the excess zipper tape from the stopper end of the zipper behind the lining.

✪ Center-Applied ✪ Zipper

You can use this basic zipper technique in a variety of removable, washable pillow covers. Once you feel confident with the process, you can make a duvet cover by enlarging the front and back and applying a very long zipper. This is also a wonderful way to use those extra quilt blocks that didn't make it into a quilt. Turn them into pillows for your sewing room or gifts for your guild.

Supplies

Zipper: 1 plastic nonseparating, 2″ longer than top edge of project, and a zipper foot for sewing machine

Seam ripper

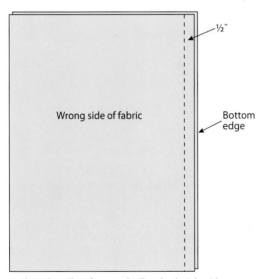

1. Place the pillow front and pillow back right sides together. Sew a ½″ seam from edge to edge along the bottom side of the pillow. Press the seam open. *Note: If your fabric is directional, pay close attention when determining the bottom edge.*

2. Unzip the zipper slightly and tack-stitch (using a wide zigzag stitch) the open end of the zipper tape to keep it from separating during installation.

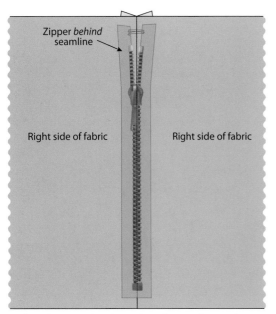

Zipper *behind* seamline

Right side of fabric

Right side of fabric

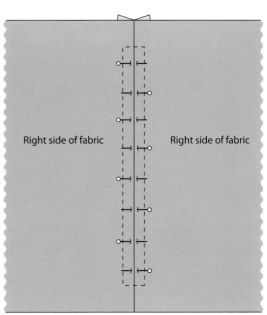

Right side of fabric

Right side of fabric

3. Place the zipper face down along the seamline on the wrong side of the pillow pieces so the zipper teeth are facing the seam allowance. Center the zipper on the seam where the planned opening will be.

4. Pin the zipper in place from the right side using straight pins. Be sure the pins go through both the seam allowances and the zipper tape. *Note: Before you begin sewing the zipper to the fabric, unzip the zipper 1″–2″ for easier opening later.*

5. Place a zipper foot on the machine. Working from the right side of the fabric, sew a rectangle shape around the zipper ¼″ from the seamline. The stitched rectangle should be centered on the seamline and should be about 2″–3″ shorter than the seam. At each short end of the rectangle, sew and then backstitch completely over the zipper teeth. Sew slowly and carefully as you travel over the zipper teeth and around the zipper-pull area. You can sew through the plastic teeth, but you cannot sew through the metal parts. Remove the pins as you sew.

6. Check the back of the seam to make sure the zipper tape is securely stitched.

7. Use a seam ripper to carefully remove the stitching line within the rectangle. This will reveal the centered zipper and the zipper pull, tucked neatly behind the folded edges of what was previously the seam.

✪ Center-Applied ✪ Zipper with Lining

This technique is ideal for any bag or purse that requires a secure, closed top edge. Though the projects in this book are based on rectangular shapes, you can certainly apply this technique to curved shapes and rounded bags as well.

Supplies

Zipper: 1 plastic nonseparating, 2″ longer than top edge of project, and a zipper foot for sewing machine

Notes ★ *If your zipper is more than 4″ shorter than the top edge of your bag, consider folding a small coordinating-fabric rectangle around each end of the zipper and stitching across it. This will cover the end of the zipper tape in the finished bag.*

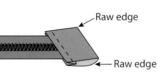

Be sure to add any embellishments, hardware, or pockets to the exterior and lining pieces before beginning to add the zipper. Add the handles too if the zipper will interfere with their positioning.

Choose a zipper in a coordinating color or a bright contrasting color. With this technique, the zipper will be exposed along the top of the bag. ★

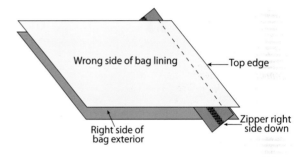

1. Place the lining and the exterior fabric right sides together. Slip the zipper in between the layers so that the right side of the zipper is facing the right side of the exterior fabric. Make sure the zipper is centered from side to side and that the edge of the zipper tape is aligned with the raw edges of the lining and exterior.

2. Using a zipper foot, sew along the entire length of the top edge with a ⅜″ seam allowance. This stitching line should be within ⅛″ of the zipper teeth. You can't see the zipper teeth as you sew, but you will be able to feel them with your fingers as you work.

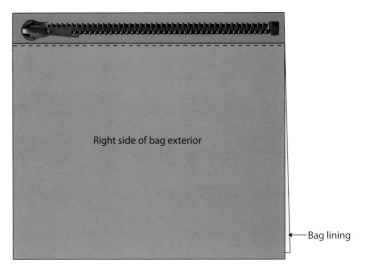

Right side of bag exterior

Bag lining

3. Open the 2 pieces of fabric to reveal the zipper. Fold the exterior and lining pieces away from the zipper teeth and press. With the exterior fabric up, edge-stitch along the seamline to hold the exterior and lining pieces in place.

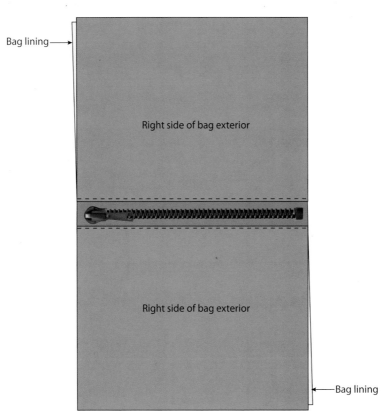

Bag lining

Right side of bag exterior

Right side of bag exterior

Bag lining

4. Sandwich the other side of the zipper tape between the remaining exterior and lining pieces; repeat Steps 1–3.

Tack stitch

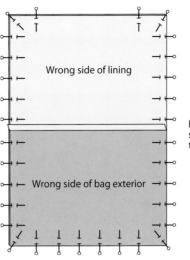

Wrong side of lining

Wrong side of bag exterior

Pin zipper tape and seam allowances toward lining.

5. Unzip the zipper slightly. Tack-stitch the open end of the zipper tapes together. *Note: You will not need to tack the zipper ends if you've applied the fabric rectangle, because it will hold the ends together.*

6. Unzip the zipper at least halfway. Place the exterior fabrics right sides together and do the same for the lining pieces. Pin around the perimeter, leaving an opening at the bottom edge of the lining. Larger bags need larger openings; smaller bags need smaller openings. When pinning the zipper area, make sure the zipper tape is pointed toward the lining side of the bag. This will take patience and careful manipulation.

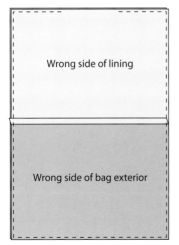

Wrong side of lining

Wrong side of bag exterior

7. Sew around the bag perimeter with a ½" seam allowance. Backstitch at the beginning and end of the stitching line and remember to leave an opening in the lining. As you approach the zipper teeth and tape, you may need to manually turn the sewing machine's handwheel to control the needle. This will help ensure that your needle doesn't break when sewing across the zipper teeth.

You can now either turn the bag right side out or add the bag-shaping darts.

Free-motion quilting designs

Layering

Spread the backing wrong side up and tape down the edges with masking tape. (If you are working on carpet, you can use T-pins to secure the backing to the carpet.) Center the batting on top, smoothing out any folds. Place the quilt top right side up on top of the batting and backing, making sure it is centered.

Basting

Basting keeps the "quilt sandwich" layers from shifting while you quilt.

Pin baste the quilt layers together with safety pins placed approximately 3″–4″ apart. Begin basting in the center and move toward the edges, first in vertical and then horizontal rows. Try not to pin directly on areas you intend to quilt.

Quilting

Quilting enhances the quilt's pieced or appliquéd design. You may choose to quilt in-the-ditch (over the seamlines), to echo the pieced or appliqué motifs, to use patterns from quilting design books and stencils, or to do your own free-motion quilting. (See the examples at left.) Remember to check the batting manufacturer's recommendations for how close the quilting lines must be.

SEWING AND QUILTING TECHNIQUES

Binding

1. Trim excess batting and backing from the quilt so they are even with the edges of the quilt top.

2. Piece binding strips together with diagonal seams to make one continuous strip. Trim the seam allowance to ¼". Press the seams open.

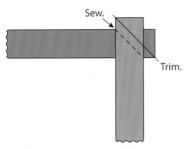

Sew from corner to corner.

Completed diagonal seam

3. Press the entire strip in half lengthwise with wrong sides together. With raw edges even, pin the binding to the front edge of the quilt a few inches away from the corner. Leave the first few inches of the binding unattached. Start sewing, using a ¼" seam allowance.

4. Stop ¼" away from the first corner (A) and backstitch 1 stitch. Lift the presser foot and needle. Rotate the quilt a quarter turn. Fold the binding so it extends straight above the quilt and the fold forms a 45° angle in the corner (B). Then fold the binding strip down even with the edge of the quilt (C). Begin sewing at the folded edge. Repeat in the same manner at all corners.

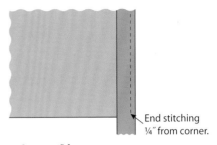

A. Sew to ¼" from corner.

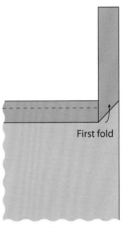

B. First fold for miter

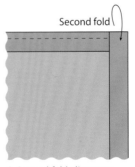

C. Second fold alignment

5. Continue sewing until you are near the beginning of the binding strip.

6. Fold under the beginning tail of the binding strip ¼" so that the raw edge will be inside the binding after it is turned to the back side of the quilt. Place the end tail of the binding strip over the beginning folded end. Continue to attach the binding and sew slightly beyond the starting stitches. Trim the excess binding. Fold the binding over the raw edges to the quilt back and hand sew, mitering the corners.

Labels

Quilt labels are very important, especially for a quilt made with someone's clothing. The label does not need to be fancy, but it should be a piece of fabric sewn to the back of the quilt. The label can include details such as who made and quilted the quilt, when it was made, for whom it was made, and if it was made in honor of someone.

Given the nature of quilts made from recycled uniforms, here's what a label might look like.

If you use a pen or a marker, make sure the ink is permanent. Another option is to use printable inkjet fabric sheets or Transfer Artist Paper (TAP, by C&T Publishing) and put your inkjet printer to use. As with any and all elements of quilting, be as creative and imaginative as you like.

You may trace or scan and print the quilt labels that follow, or you can find more labels in the *Quilt Label Collective CD—Volume I* (by C&T Publishing), which is available at your local quilt or craft store or from www.ctpub.com.

> *Made from your daddy's uniform*
> *Captain Matthew Morello*
> *Joint Base Balad,*
> *Iraq 6/20/2010–11/04/2010*
> *For: Aubrey*
> *Quilt by: Jen Eskridge*
> *Quilting by: Colleen Eskridge*
> *Completed: January 2011*

THANK YOU

For Aubrey

Made from Daddy's Uniforms
Capt. Matt Morello
Joint Air Base Balad, Iraq
June 2010 – November 2010

Quilt by Jen Eskridge
Machine Quilting by Colleen Eskridge
February 2011

TEMPLATE PATTERNS

Tree Skirt Center Circle
Use at this size.

Circle Purse Pattern
Enlarge 200%.
Cut 2 exterior fabric.
Cut 2 lining fabric.
Cut 2 batting.
Cut 2 interfacing.
Cut 2 pocket fabric.

Center

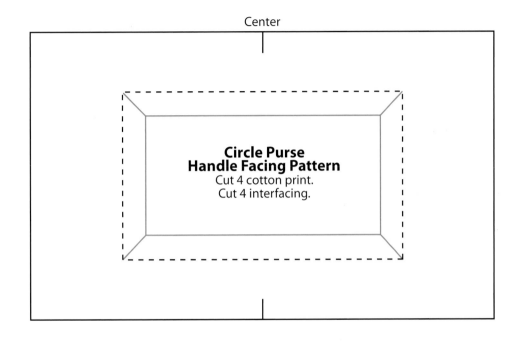

**Circle Purse
Handle Facing Pattern**
Cut 4 cotton print.
Cut 4 interfacing.

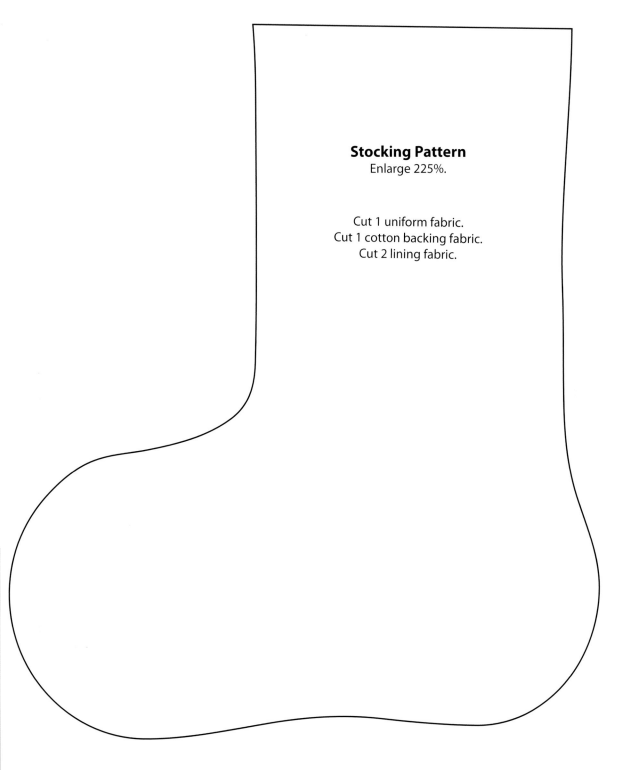

Stocking Pattern
Enlarge 225%.

Cut 1 uniform fabric.
Cut 1 cotton backing fabric.
Cut 2 lining fabric.

TEMPLATE PATTERNS

Half-Moon Purse Pattern
Enlarge 125%.

Zipper placement
(lining only)

Place on fold.

TEMPLATE PATTERNS

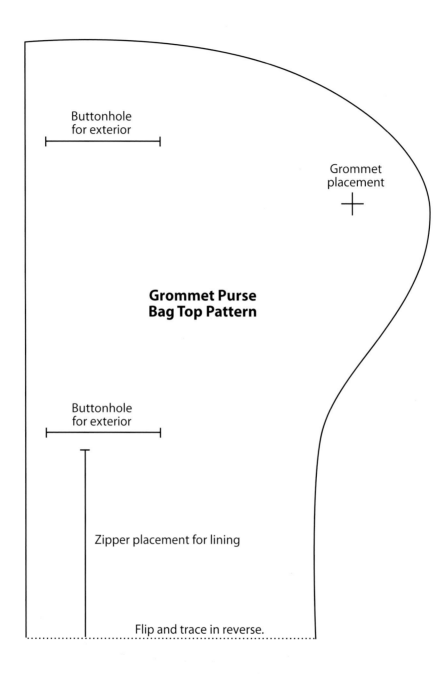

Buttonhole
for exterior

Grommet
placement

Grommet Purse
Bag Top Pattern

Buttonhole
for exterior

Zipper placement for lining

Flip and trace in reverse.

TEMPLATE PATTERNS

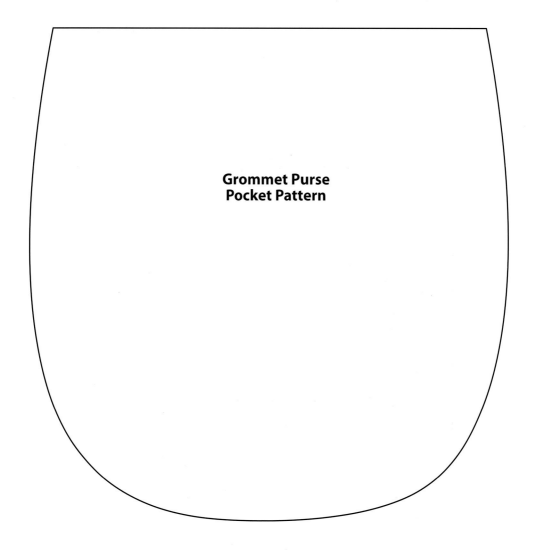

**Grommet Purse
Pocket Pattern**

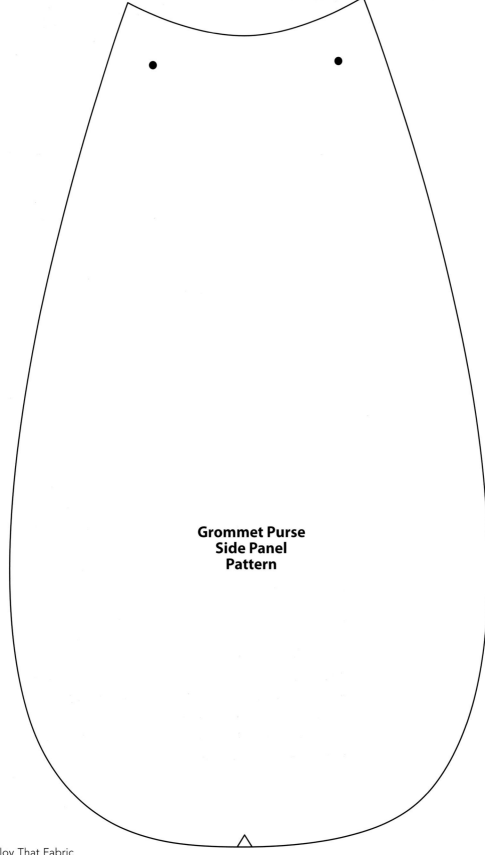

Grommet Purse
Side Panel
Pattern

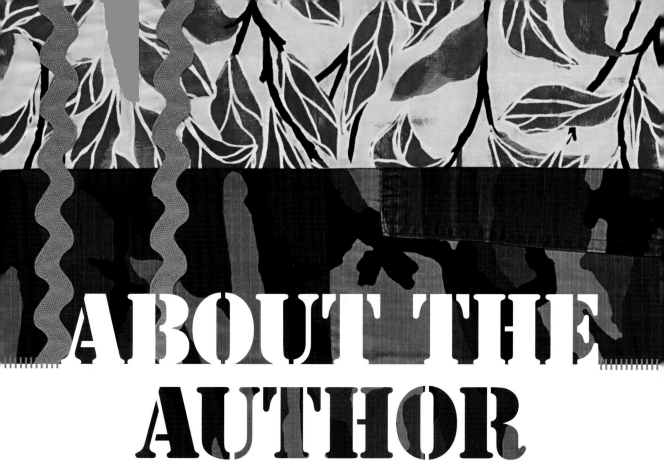

ABOUT THE AUTHOR

Photo by Julie Gamez

Designer Jen Eskridge has been quilting for fifteen years and sewing for a bit longer. She is a military spouse to a fabulous guy currently on active duty in the Kansas Air National Guard. While he was active with the U.S. Air Force, Jen had the opportunity to live in five different cities in ten years, including living on a military base in Daegu, South Korea.

Jen graduated from Louisiana State University in 1998 with an apparel design degree, which she uses daily while working on quilting and sewing patterns for her company, ReannaLily Designs. The company launched the Seamingly Accurate Seam Guide in October 2008. Since then, ReannaLily Designs has published many patterns, including the first Recycled Uniform Pattern— The Cube Purse—released in October 2009. Read more at www.reannalilydesigns.com.

For a list of other fine books from C&T Publishing, visit our website to view our catalog online.

C&T PUBLISHING, INC.
P.O. Box 1456
Lafayette, CA 94549
800-284-1114

Email: ctinfo@ctpub.com
Website: www.ctpub.com

C&T Publishing's professional photography services are now available to the public. Visit us at www.ctmediaservices.com.

Tips and Techniques can be found at www.ctpub.com > Consumer Resources > Quiltmaking Basics: Tips & Techniques for Quiltmaking & More

For quilting supplies:

COTTON PATCH
1025 Brown Ave.
Lafayette, CA 94549
Store: 925-284-1177
Mail order: 925-283-7883

Email: CottonPa@aol.com
Website: www.quiltusa.com

Note: Fabrics used in the quilts shown may not be currently available, as fabric manufacturers keep most fabrics in print for only a short time.